YOUNG REED

Encyclopedia of
Australian Animals

Published in 2023 by New Holland Publishers
Sydney

First published in Australia in 2008 by Young Reed
An imprint of New Holland Publishers
Sydney

Level 1, 178 Fox Valley Road, Wahroonga, NSW 2076, Australia

newhollandpublishers.com

Copyright © 2023 New Holland Publishers
Copyright © 2023 in text: Martyn Robinson
Copyright © 2023 in photographs: As credited this page

All rights reserved. No part of this publication may be reproduced,
stored in a retrieval system or transmitted, in any form or by any
means, electronic, mechanical, photocopying, recording or
otherwise, without the prior written permission of the publishers
and copyright holders.

A record of this book is held at the National Library of Australia.

10 9 8 7 6 5 4 3 2 1

ISBN 9781921580543

Managing Director: Fiona Schultz
Commissioning Editor: Yani Silvana
Editor: Shelley Barons
Project Editor: Jenny Scepanovic
Designer: Andrew Davies
Production Director: Arlene Gippert
Printed in China

Keep up with New Holland Publishers:
 NewHollandPublishers
 @newhollandpublishers

Picture credits
t = top, c = centre, b = bottom
Andrew Davies 102b
Becca Saunders: 40b, 41t, 44b, 53t, 53b, 77t, 78, 79t, 80t, 80b,
81t, 81b, 84, 85b, 104t, 105, 106, 108t, 109, 121
Ken Griffiths: 8b, 9c, 14, 15t, 13t, 17t, 18, 21b, 29b, 30, 38b, 40b,
47b, 47c, 50, 51t, 51b, 54t, 59, 60b, 74b, 75, 77b, 95t, 103t, 103b,
110, 111b, 125t
Lochman Transparencies: 6–7, 8t, 9t, 9b, 11t, 11b, 12, 13b, 15b, 16,
19, 20, 21t, 22, 23, 24, 25tr, 25tl, 25b, 26, 27t, 27b, 28t, 28b, 29t,
31t, 31b, 32, 33t, 34, 35tr, 35b, 36, 37t, 37b, 41b, 39t, 39b, 45b,
46, 47t, 49t, 49b, 52, 54b, 55t, 55b, 56, 57t, 57b, 58, 60t, 61, 62,
63t, 63b, 64, 65, 66, 67t, 67b, 69t, 69b, 74t, 76, 79b, 82, 83t, 86,
88, 89t, 89b, 90, 92t, 92b, 93t, 94t, 94b, 96, 97, 98, 99t, 99b, 100,
101t, 101c, 101b, 11t, 112t, 112b, 113, 114t, 115t, 115b, 122t,
123, 125b
NHIL: 10b, 17b, 33b, 35c, 42, 43t, 43b, 44t, 45t, 73b, 68, 70, 71,
72, 83b, 87, 89c, 91t, 93b, 95b, 99c, 102t, 107, 116, 118, 119
Queensland Museum: 10t
Shutterstock: 73t, 85t, 104b, 108b, 114b, 117, 120, 122b

YOUNG REED

Encyclopedia
of
AUSTRALIAN
ANIMALS

Martyn Robinson

young
reed

Contents

Outback Australia

The Great Southern Land

Australia is an unusual place. It is classed as an Island Continent, as it is surrounded by water (that's what 'girt by sea' means!). It isn't connected to any other large land masses from which animals could easily migrate. As a result, a large proportion of our plants and animals have evolved here, isolated from the rest of the world. There are many animal and plant species that are found ONLY in Australia and nowhere else. Some have their closest relatives here and nowhere else; and some were once widespread globally, but have died out everywhere else.

Australia is famous for its marsupials and monotremes. In fact, Australia and New Guinea are the only countries where egg-laying mammals still exist. There are also quite a few native Australian placental mammals, such as the dingo and some species of bats and rodents. Our marine fauna is just as diverse, and our fresh water fauna contains many unique surprises, such as the Queensland Lungfish. Birdlife in Australia is abundant and colourful. We boast an amazing number of parrots and cockatoos; the second and third largest birds alive today; nectar-feeding species; the world's smallest penguin and largest cuckoos and kingfishers.

The environment, including plant life, determines what animals live in a particular area, and our native plants are just as diverse and unique as the animals. Many animals have evolved with a special relationship with certain plants. For example Australia has a great many plant species pollinated by birds rather than insects, as birds can often survive hot dry conditions that might kill bees or butterflies. Bird-pollinated flowers are usually red and have little scent. This is to deter bees, which are red-green colour blind, but have a good sense of smell.

Australia has all of this and yet is also one of the driest, most nutrient-poor countries on Earth. Our plants and animals are built to survive all the harsh conditions the country can generate, but sadly many cannot survive the additional pressures we humans place on them: habitat destruction, increased salination, and competition with introduced species. Australia is an unusual place!

Habitats and Environments

Australia has many types of environments that contain many more habitats. An environment is the surroundings and broad area that an animal inhabits, containing all that it needs and all that affects it. An example of an environment is temperate coastal waters. A habitat is the more immediate surroundings of an animal within the environment, or where it normally lives or can be expected to be found. Examples of habitats within the temperate coastal waters environment are kelp forests, sea grass beds and sandy beaches, depending on the animal. Within each environment there are many habitats.

The dry desert environment

Desert survivors

Deserts and arid lands lack the essential requirements animals need to live – mainly abundant water. Animals and plants living in these arid zones must be able to survive extremely hot, dry conditions. Most have evolved special features to help them survive with little water.

Rainforests rich in life

Tropical rainforests are important Australian environments that are often nutrient-poor areas, struggling to grow on sand and slowly building up and recycling materials necessary for life in the bodies of its inhabitants – from both living and dead. There is usually a diverse range of animals in these areas as the 'slim pickings' means that everything must struggle to find food and all have an equal chance. Stronger or faster breeding species can't dominate the environment.

Damp rainforest

Tall timber in a Eucalypt forest

Freshwater rivers and lakes

Australian freshwater rivers, lakes and wetlands can have very different conditions. They can be in drought – where the rivers may dry to a series of small unconnected pools – or they can flood – where the rivers overflow their banks and cover wide areas called floodplains. Animals living in these environments must be able to survive these extremes. They are often good swimmers or very mobile.

The Great Southern Ocean

Eucalypt forests

This is the dominant forest type in Australia, characterised by open spaces, which allow lots of light and air to circulate. They may be hot and dry in summer but the hard, vertically-hanging leaves reduce water loss for the plants. Eucalypts have many species which retain their leaves (evergreens), but shed their bark annually. Both leaves and bark contain eucalyptus oil and are quick to burn, making Eucalypt forests prone to bushfires. Many plants rely on the fire to germinate their seeds. The animals that live here must have bushfire survival tactics too.

An inland river in drought

Australia's south coast

The southern oceans are usually very rich in animal life due to upwelling currents – water from near the ocean floor rises to the surface bringing sediment that helps plant plankton to grow. But the water is also cooler, which affects the growth of many animals that cannot maintain their own body temperature. There are a lot more of the smaller cold-blooded animals here than the larger ones. Huge whales, seals and the larger species of penguins live closer to Antarctica and feed on large numbers of tiny krill and fish.

Classifying Animals

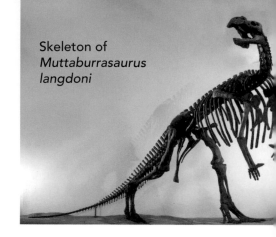

Skeleton of *Muttaburrasaurus langdoni*

As you look through this book you might notice a number of scientific terms and words. They may be words that you've never heard before and look difficult to pronounce, but they're there for a purpose. Most of these big words have to do with how we classify animals. If you're interested in dinosaurs, these words may look familiar, as they're usually Latin or Ancient Greek, just like *Tyrannosaurus rex*, *Muttaburrasaurus langdoni* and *Stegosaurus stenops* – which are also the scientific names of animals.

Dacelo novaeguineae

Living things are grouped according to their common features. These groupings range from broad ones, like kingdoms (for example animals, plants), to narrow ones, like species (for example Laughing Kookaburra *Dacelo novaeguineae*, Southern Stingless Bee *Trigona carbonaria*). The more features they have in common, the more closely related they are. The scientific name of a species is always written in italics or underlined to make it clear that this is its official name in any language. The genus name, which comes first, always starts with a capital and the species name is always lower case, even if it includes someone's name. There may be several species in a genus. For example, in the genus *Dacelo* – the kookaburras – there are four species: Laughing Kookaburra (*Dacelo novaeguineae*), Spangled Kookaburra (*Dacelo tyro*), Rufus-bellied Kookaburra (*Dacelo gaudichaud*) and Blue-winged Kookaburra (*Dacelo leachii*).

Why Latin and Ancient Greek?

Well, it was decided long ago that if the scientific names were to be universally accepted and used by scientists all over the world, then the terms must be in a language that wouldn't be confusing to anyone by being part of an existing language – therefore it had to be in a language that was either dead or invented. As both Latin and Ancient Greek were sufficiently different to their modern day counterparts, they were chosen. As time has gone on, Latinised versions of people's names have been used e.g. the species name *robinsoni* would be named after someone called Robinson.

Classifying a humble mouse

Using a House Mouse (*Mus musculus*) as an example, a full classification of an animal would be:

Kingdom Animalia – all living organisms that are made of more than just a single cell.

Phylum Chordata – all animals that have a notochord (a hollow dorsal nerve chord) at some stage of life.

Subphylum Vertebrata – (more specific than a phylum, but less specific than a class) all animals with a backbone.

Class Mammalia (Mammals) – all animals that have warm blood, produce milk to feed their young, and have hair (even whales!).

Subclass Eutheria or Placentals – Mammals are divided into three subclasses: Placentals, Marsupials and Monotremes. Eutheria or Placentals are mammals that give birth to live young, which develop inside the mother with a placenta, which passes nutrients and removes waste from the young via the mother's bloodstream.

Order Rodentia – placental mammals that have an upper and lower pair of constantly growing incisor teeth, and nipples along their bellies rather than only on their chests.

Family Muridae – rodents with excellent hearing and sense of smell, but poorer vision. All have slender, scaled tails and almost all have naked young at birth.

Genus *Mus* – small, tailed rodents living mainly on seeds and resembling small rats,

Want to know how to pronounce those big scientific names?

Try *Ornithorhynchus anatinus*! It looks impossible at first, but breaking it up into syllables makes it easier. Try saying this:

Or–nee–thor–ink–us an–at–in–us.

If you managed that, you've just said the scientific name for the Platypus.

Ornithorhynchus anatinus

with a notch on the chisel-like surface of the upper incisor teeth.

Species *Mus musculus* – all the features mentioned above, plus this is the only rodent in Australia with the notched upper incisor teeth and five pairs of nipples along the belly of the females.

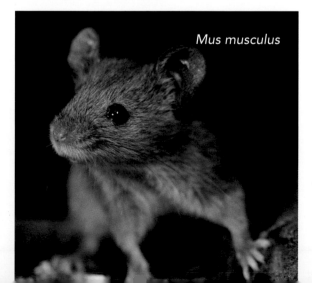

Mus musculus

nts

Ants are found everywhere on Earth, except on Antarctica. Ants are arthropod insects belonging to the Formicidae family. They are close relatives of wasps and bees, which is why many of them can sting. Their jointed legs, sensitive antennae and tough exoskeletons have made them very successful animals.

Meat-eating ants

Meat or Gravel Ants (*Iridomyrmex purpureus*) build large nests, covering the entrance area with pebbles. They are fond of meat and have been used for cleaning bones. Often several nests in an area are related and trails can be worn in the ground from steady streams of ants running between nests or out to foraging areas and back. The ants like sweet nectar from flowers and honeydew-producing insects but also catch small animals to feed their grubs.

Atomic ants

Always frantically busy, some ants can run around in the hot sun all day and never run out of energy. Many have radiation-proof bodies and would survive the effects of a nuclear blast better than cockroaches or people! Being social insects, ants are very efficient foragers, co-operating to find food and bring it back for the whole colony to share.

Meat Ants drinking from a puddle

Green Tree-Ants
in their silk nest

Building with babies

Green Tree-Ants (*Oecophylla smaragdina*) use their babies like tubes of glue! Most ant larvae possess silk glands to spin a cocoon to pupate in, but these ants use this ant-grub silk to make their nests. Groups of worker ants haul two leaf edges together while other workers grab a larva with full silk glands and squeeze out the liquid silk to glue the two leaf surfaces together. When that grub is empty they put it back in the pile and pick up another full one to continue. Also called Green Weaver-Ants these unusual ants build nests up in trees in tropical Australia, where they live. They are voracious predators that ambush other insects, spiders and even baby birds and small lizards.

Jumping Jack flash

The Jack Jumper is probably the world's most dangerous species of ant – several people have died from its sting. This is because many people have a violent allergic reaction to its venom, just as some people are terribly allergic to bee stings. The Jack Jumper is a small species of bull-ant, which is black with yellow jaws. As its name suggests, it jumps at prey and attackers – including innocent people!

Jack Jumper Ant

Arachnids

Arachnids are a class of arthropods that have eight legs, and often have venom glands. The class includes spiders, scorpions, ticks, mites, and some less well known groups, such as harvestmen, whip-spiders, whip-scorpions and false-scorpions. Spiders are unique in having both venom glands and silk-producing glands. Scorpions have a venomous stinger and ticks have potentially toxic saliva. Most arachnids are predators on smaller invertebrate animals, but some also feed on plant matter.

Glow in the dark

For some reason, scorpions fluoresce under ultraviolet light, glowing greenish or purple, making them easily collected at night by arachnologists and desert researchers.

Scary scorpion mums

Although scorpions can give a painful sting, none of the Australian species is considered dangerous to humans. Scorpions have a pair of crab-like claws, or pedipalps, at the front of the body, followed by four pairs of legs, ending in a long segmented tail with a stinger at the tip. Surprisingly, scorpions make good mothers and after giving birth to a number of live young, the female carries them around on her back until they can fend for themselves.

The Black-Rock Scorpion is common around Canberra

Funnelweb Spider

The male of the Sydney Funnelweb Spider is the most dangerous venomous spider in the world. Luckily, due to an antivenom, no-one has died since the 1980s. These spiders are common along Sydney's northern shore region, but as far north as Newcastle, west as Lithgow and south as Nowra and can be found in damp areas particularly under rocks or logs. They feed on a variety of ground- dwelling invertebrates.

Male Sydney Funnelweb

Bush Tick

Bush Tick

The Bush Tick (*Haemaphysalis longicornis*) is an introduced species thought to have been accidentally brought to Australia from Japan. Currently it seems to be restricted to the eastern and western coastal areas of Australia. The Bush Tick is commonly found on domestic livestock and dogs but will attack humans as well. Strangely it hasn't been recorded as attacking any native mammals – perhaps it doesn't like marsupial blood?

Arthropods

Insects, crustaceans, centipedes, millipedes, spiders and scorpions are all arthropods – the largest phylum of the animal kingdom. They don't have a skeleton inside, like you and me. Instead, they have one on the outside, called an exoskeleton. Animals without internal skeletons are called invertebrates. Arthropods also have jointed limbs rather like ours, with numerous 'knees', 'wrists' and 'elbows'. They can be found all over the place: on land, in trees, flying in the air, underwater and underground.

Velvet Worm or *Peripatus*

Velvety or slimy?

Velvet worms are the missing link between the jointed-legged arthropods, such as insects, and the soft-bodied worms, such as annelids. They are predators who catch their prey and defend themselves in an unusual way. Running the length of their body are two 'slime glands'. Jets of this sticky slime are squirted from nozzles at the side of their head at prey, to glue it to the ground, and at predators, to gum them up. Fossils resembling velvet worms have been found dating back about 500 million years.

Bark-Mimic Grasshopper

Hopping mad

Most grasshoppers don't live in, or eat, grass and many prefer to scurry rather than hop! Even the most famous of all the grasshoppers – the plague locusts – do most of their damage by flying into an area then dropping out of the sky to feast on any plant matter – not just grass. If they're hungry enough they've even been known to eat green- coloured cotton clothing hanging on the washing line! Some species do live in and feed on grasses and these have given the group (order Orthoptera) their common name.

Crazy crabs

The Australian Land Hermit Crab (*Coenobita variabilis*) is found across northern Australia in coastal areas. By day it shelters under beach sand or cavities in mangroves and forests and at night, and sometimes on overcast days, it scurries about on the surface looking for things to eat. And there's not much it won't try: dead leaves, twigs and bark, animal dung, human garbage and even dead and dying animals. As the hermit crab grows it sheds its skin and finds ever larger shells to live in.

The Strawberry Hermit Crab (*Coenobita perlatus*) is a tropical relative of the Australian Land Hermit Crab.

andicoots and Bilbies

The word 'bandicoot' is Indian – not Australian – and refers to a species of large rat. Early settlers familiar with these Indian rats thought they resembled the marsupials seen around the bushland and gave them the same name – but they are unrelated. Our bandicoots are marsupials with different biology and lifestyle to the rodent bandicoots of India.

The Bilby is sometimes known as the Rabbit-eared Bandicoot

Hoppin' down the bilby trail

Bilbies do not need to drink at all. They get all the moisture they need from their food: fungi, fallen fruit, bulbs, roots and seeds, as well as insects, spiders and lizards. Like other bandicoots, Bilbies have a very short gestation – just 12 days. Their long rabbit-like ears have led to them being promoted as an Australian alternative to the Easter Bunny (an introduced species!). The smaller Lesser Bilby became extinct around the 1950s as a result of habitat destruction and introduced predators.

A handy pest controller

The Long-nosed Bandicoot (*Perameles nasuta*) is a Funnelweb Spider's nightmare! It is immune to the spiders' venom and loves eating them. These nocturnal animals do a lot of good in lawns and gardens even though they are often cursed for the little conical holes they leave. The bandicoots make the holes when digging up mole crickets, lawn grubs, cut-worms and other garden pests. You can watch these creatures at night using a torch covered in red cellophane, as they cannot see red.

Mysterious northerners

The Spiny Bandicoot (*Echymipera rufescens*) is found in the northern Cape York Peninsula, further north than Cooktown, and in New Guinea. It is fairly common in the dense forested areas but has also been found in nearby grasslands and woodlands. There is little known about this creature, probably because of its habitat. It eats insects as well as some vegetable matter and fungi.

The lone Quenda

The Southern Brown Bandicoot, or Quenda (*Isoodon obesulus*), is widespread across southern Australia, but numbers have dramatically declined, due to introduced foxes, feral cats and habitat destruction. Quendas live among dense vegetation, which provides both tricky hiding places and lots of yummy food. Buried food is dug up with their sharp claws, leaving distinctive cone-shaped holes in the earth. Quendas are solitary and nocturnal and spend the day in oval nests built from leaves and dirt.

Southern Brown Bandicoot or Quenda (*Isoodon obesulus*)

Bats

Bats are the only flying mammals, although several others can glide. Bat wings are formed from extended 'webbed' fingers, which connect to their ankles, rather like the fabric on an umbrella. Bats are placental mammals and are divided into two groups: Microchiroptera – the little insect-eating bats, which use echolocation and have webbing extending to their tails as well; and Megachiroptera – larger flying foxes and fruit bats, which use sight and smell for navigation and have little or no tail.

The False Vampire or Ghost Bat is a predator

That vampire's fake

The False Vampire Bat is Australia's largest insectivorous bat – and it doesn't just stick to insects! These bats will drop onto sleeping birds, lizards, frogs and small rodents – even other bats caught in flight – and carry them off to a roost where they can be dismembered and eaten in safety. You can spot these roosts by the grisly sight of the discarded wings, legs and heads of their victims, littering the ground below. Due to their pale grey or white colouring, they are also known as Ghost Bats.

Hearing dinner in the dark

Insect-eating bats use sound to 'see' in the dark. This is called echolocation. The bats make high-pitched sounds, which bounce back as echoes when the sound waves strike any objects in front of the bat. The sooner the echo is heard, the closer the object is. So the bat can catch it if it is food, or avoid it if it is a tree trunk or building! This system is so well developed that bats can tell one species of insect from another by echo alone.

A nose like a horseshoe

Horseshoe bats have one of the strangest noses in the animal world. Shaped like a horseshoe, the strange leaf-like flaps of skin around the bat's nose are used to concentrate sound waves in a particular direction, giving them more control. As a result, Horseshoe bats can carefully examine tree trunks and rocky outcrops using echolocation to find hidden insects. They are very nimble fliers and can zip in and out of confined spaces and among rocks and trees without crashing.

Cute as a blossom

One relative of the flying fox is the tiny mouse-sized Blossom Bat of the tropical rainforests. Blossom Bats have a tongue like a toothbrush to collect nectar and pollen from flowers.

The Eastern Horseshoe Bat emits sound through its nose

Foxy relatives

Some Australian flying foxes have a wingspan of over a metre. Although classed with bats, some scientists think that flying foxes and their batty relatives are only similar due to 'convergent evolution'. This is where animals with a similar way of life closely resemble one another despite being unrelated. All flying foxes use their large eyes, sensitive noses and mobile ears to find their way about, rather than the echolocation used by insect-eating bats. Flying foxes feed on fruit, nectar and pollen in the forests of north and east Australia.

Flying foxes help spread the seeds of rainforest trees

Bees

Bees are close relatives of ants and wasps – which makes them Hymenopterans, insects and arthropods. Adults and young feed almost exclusively on pollen and nectar from flowers collected on the branched hairs covering their bodies of the adults. Most species can sting and many are social insects, forming colonies in a hive.

Bees in blue

Unlike honey bees that live in large colonies, beautiful blue-banded bees are solitary, meaning they live alone, but will often have close neighbours. These bees burrow a nest underground or in soft sandstone. Blue-banded bees (*Amegilla* sp.) are expert pollinators and use a special method that involves holding the flowers and buzzing. This sound and movement makes the pollen drop from the flower onto the bee. Blue-banded bees love the colour blue! Their favourite flowers are blue and purple.

A Blue-banded Bee

Stingless bees guarding
their nest entrance

Stingless bee

Australian native bees that produce honey
cannot sting, but their honey, called 'sugarbag',
is especially tasty. Because wild stingless bees
only produce a small amount of honey, methods
have been developed to keep and breed many
stingless bee species in artificial hives, and to
harvest their honey without damaging the
colony. The hive structure is very different to the
introduced honeybees, as the stingless bees
don't have vertical combs.

Stingless, but not defenceless!

In Mexico, stingless bees are known
as 'hair twisters'. If a colony is attacked,
each bee will fly at the attacker and bite
onto whatever it can – in mammals,
including humans, this is usually hair,
anywhere on the body – and try to
twist or pull it out! This is a very
effective defence against
most nest raiders.

Beetles

There are more species of beetle than any other type of insect. Beetles clearly are a very successful order of insects (order Coleoptera, meaning 'covered wings'). All beetles start life as grubs or larvae, often feeding on a different food to the adults. They then pupate, like a butterfly, before emerging as adult beetles.

Long live the beetle

Some beetles live in deserts, others on beaches, in fresh water, underground, under bark, even in the bodies of living animals. Some beetles live for a matter of months, while others can last for several years.

Christmas beetles

Christmas beetles are a variety of scarab beetle, commonly seen in December – hence the name. On warm summer nights they can be seen flying around outdoor lights. Adult beetles feed on the leaves of eucalypts and, in large numbers, can defoliate a tree in no time at all. In years past, only the brightly coloured beetles with metallic iridescent wings were called Christmas beetles – but these have become rare, possibly due to habitat destruction. Nowadays the name is given to almost any big beetle that shows up around Christmas time!

Christmas beetles come in a variety of colours

Longicorn beetles have boring grubs

The Piedish Beetle lives in arid Australia

Boring beetles

Borers are wood-tunnelling insect larvae. They are mostly beetle or moth larvae, which bore through living or dead timber, feeding as they grow. They emerge as adult insects to mate and seek out new timber, in which to lay eggs. Although regarded as pests in forestry, agricultural and furniture industries, most borers seem to seek out timber that is unhealthy, or already dead, to tunnel in, and they really only speed up the natural death or decomposition of the plant. Witjuti grubs are a type of borer.

All sorts of beetles

There are over 350,000 beetle species worldwide and at least 20,000 in Australia. Beetles are a varied bunch, eating from a wide menu: leaves, nectar, pollen, other insects, rotting meat, dung, detritus, wood and fungus. Beetles are chewers, some with surprisingly strong jaws, enabling them to eat seeds, tough hide and leather or wood.

Ladybird

Ladybirds are actually beetles and most are considered the gardener's friend. Both adults and their grub-like larvae feed on garden pests such as aphids, scale insects, thrips, psyllids and mealy bugs. Typically we think of ladybirds as being red or orange with black spots, but some are all one colour, without spots, and some species are just plain black. Each species has its favourite type of prey; there is even a vegetarian ladybird – the 28-Spotted Ladybird – which can be a pest in vegetable gardens!

Bettongs and other Rat-kangaroos

Bettongs and their relatives are also called rat-kangaroos because of their size – although most are more like rabbit size! There are five species of rat-kangaroo known as bettongs and another six if we include the potoroos and musky rat-kangaroos. They construct nests in secluded spots on the ground or in burrows. Bettongs carry nesting material in their furry prehensile tails, proving they are related to possums as well as the larger kangaroos.

The rowdy Rufous

Rufous Bettongs (*Aeprymnus rufescens*) are quite noisy animals and growl, stamp their feet and kick at one another when fighting. This rat-kangaroo species lives along the northern half of eastern Australia and along the middle of the NSW/Victorian border. It feeds on grasses, herbs, roots and tubers and fungi. As well as native predators, the introduced fox and habitat destruction are the main threats to their survival.

A baby Burrowing Bettong or Boodie

Burrowing Boodies

Boodies, also known as Burrowing Bettongs, are the only kangaroo-like species that live in burrows all year round. They were once one of the most abundant and widespread marsupials on mainland Australia, so common they were regarded as pests. Now extinct on the mainland, they are found naturally only on some offshore islands in Western Australia. However, boodies have been reintroduced to some protected areas they once inhabited and are currently doing well. The main threats to their survival are introduced cats and foxes.

The Long-nosed Potoroo is usually found around thick vegetation in south-eastern Australia

Storing food for later

The Musky Rat-kangaroo (*Hypsiprymnodon moschatus*) is one of only a few marsupials that is active by day. These inhabitants of the north Queensland rainforests eat insects and fungi as well as fallen rainforest fruits. They sometimes bury fruit and seeds in the forest floor to be dug up and eaten later, but they often forget where these are and end up accidentally 'planting' new trees. Although the population is reduced due to human activity it is still quite common in certain areas.

New potoroos

Even though potoroos have very short back legs (compared to others in the rat-kangaroo family) these bandicoot-like animals still prefer to hop rather than run. There were four species of potoroo at the time of European settlement, but the Broad-faced Potoroo was already rare and is now thought to be extinct. One species, the Long-footed Potoroo, was quite recently discovered – recognised as a new species in 1978. Another species, Gilbert's Potoroo, was rediscovered in 1994, after being thought extinct for 120 years.

Woylie

The Woylie or Brush-tailed Bettong (*Bettongia pencillata*) sadly now occurs only in a few areas of Western Australia, but they have been reintroduced to some of the areas they once inhabited after these were cleared of the introduced foxes and feral cats that eat them. Woylies have a broad diet including seeds, roots, insects and grasses but the bulk of their diet seems to be underground fungi which are dug up at night with their strong claws.

The Woylie or Brush-tailed Bettong was once very common and widespread but is now rare

Birds of the Bush

Australian bird life is amazingly diverse, colourful and often noisy. Australia's best known bird – the Laughing Kookaburra – is a species of kingfisher. There are several native pigeon species. Some can live in very arid areas, shuttling from feeding sites to waterholes each day. Others live in the rainforest or woodlands. The warble of a Magpie after the rain is a classic Aussie bush sound.

Squeaky treats

Wonga Pigeons spend most of the day on the ground looking for food, but nest only high up in the trees. This is because they are large and tasty – a fact early settlers and introduced foxes soon discovered. So tasty, in fact, that they have disappeared from parts of their original range. Wongas are most common in rainforests and coastal scrub, but can be seen in backyards too. Their monotonous call sounds like a squeaky pump and you may be convinced that there is some sort of rusty machinery running in nearby bushland until you discover the identity of the caller!

The Wonga Pigeon has an unusual call that sounds like a squeaky pump

The Torres Strait Pigeon can eat fruits we would find poisonous

Torres Strait Pigeon

This is a large mainly white native pigeon, found in New Guinea and Indonesia, as well as northern Australia. The pigeons migrate to Australia during their breeding season, from August through to January. Considered a delicacy by many, they are wary birds, usually sheltering for the night on offshore islands or in mangroves and visiting the mainland during the day to feed on rainforest fruits. Their nest is an untidy platform of twigs and sticks built in the mangrove branches.

Merry king of the bush

Kookaburras are the world's largest kingfishers, famous for their call, which sounds like human laughter. Interestingly this distinctive sound was recorded in the past and used in movie soundtracks. Listen out for the kookaburra in some old Tarzan movies! There are two species of kookaburra in Australia: the Laughing Kookaburra and its tropical relative, the Blue-winged Kookaburra. The Blue-winged species also laughs, but sounds a bit more 'hysterical' than humorous. Laughing Kookaburras form family groups, which all cooperate to raise the chicks.

Laughing Kookaburra

The distinctive warble of the magpie is a common sound in Australian gardens

Swooping in springtime

Australian Magpies are bold birds that have learned to live alongside humans for the benefits provided: free food hand-outs; scraps scavenged from picnic sites; worms and grubs dug up in suburban lawns. During spring, however, certain areas become notorious for the nest defence by parent magpies, who swoop on anyone passing. In most cases, the magpies never make physical contact, but the swooping bird with its clacking beak can be quite frightening. Luckily these attacks usually cease once the chicks have fledged and left the nest.

Eyes in the back of your head

Magpies are less likely to swoop if they think you're watching them. Try painting eyes on top of your hat or bike helmet, or wear your sunglasses on the back of your head as you pass nesting sites to fool them!

Birds of Prey

'Birds of prey' is the term given to birds with hooked beaks and strong clawed feet for tearing apart prey. This includes hawks, falcons and eagles. All species feed on meat – either caught fresh, or as carrion.

Check out the wingspan!

Wedge-tailed Eagles are Australia's largest bird of prey and one of the world's largest eagles, with a wingspan of 2.3 metres! Its sheer size enables it to catch such large prey as wallabies and young kangaroos, but it is equally happy with carrion and often cleans up road kill or animal carcasses in drought-stricken areas. Its numbers have been maintained since the introduction of rabbits, which are a tasty and plentiful snack. Eagles make huge stick nests in the tallest trees available, and lay up to three eggs, although usually only one chick will survive. Once fully grown, Wedge-tailed Eagles can live for decades.

Wedge-tailed Eagle

Crested Hawk

Crested Hawks or Pacific Bazas (*Aviceda subcristata*) are insect specialists. Although they will occasionally eat small birds and mammals – and even tree frogs or fruit – their main diet is large insects, which they find by searching carefully among the tree canopies. Stick insects are a favourite. Pacific Bazas are easy to recognise as they are the only Australian hawk with a crest like a cockatoo, a boldly striped chest and a bright yellow eye.

The Crested Hawk is found in the forests of north and east Australia

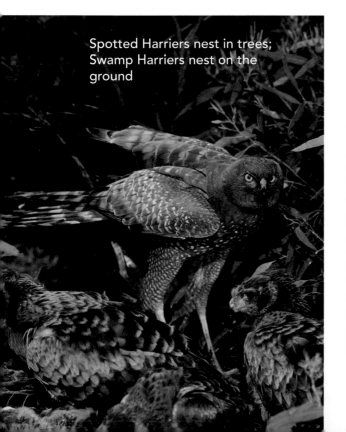

Spotted Harriers nest in trees; Swamp Harriers nest on the ground

Pirates of prey

The Australian or White-bellied Sea Eagle is the second largest bird of prey in Australia. It is found around the coast and inland, on large rivers. Although feeding mainly on fish and carrion washed up on the shore, sea eagles will also eat water birds and mammals. Living prey is snatched from the water surface or just below it, but sea eagles will also attempt to rob other birds of their catch if the opportunity arises – going so far as to force weaker birds to regurgitate already swallowed fish!

What an annoying bird

Harriers are long-legged hawks, named for the way they hunt. Usually, harriers swoop onto smaller prey like ground-dwelling birds, reptiles, insects and small mammals, their long legs snatching prey from tall grass and swampy land. However, if a harrier decides to go for something bigger, such as a rabbit or duck, it will follow the prey relentlessly, constantly driving it from cover (or underwater in the case of ducks) until the animal is exhausted and an easy target. This hunting method is called harrying.

ugs

All bugs are insects, but not all insects are bugs! In order to qualify as a 'bug', the animal must be an arthropod in the class Insecta and in the order Hemiptera (half wing). Juvenile bugs resemble the adults in appearance and diet, feeding on the same food in the same way.

Norfolk Island Hibiscus Bugs – one female and four males

A colourful warning

Harlequin bugs are brightly coloured hemipterans, which feed on the sap of a variety of plants. The Norfolk Island Hibiscus Bug, for example, feeds on hibiscus plants. The orange females lay clusters of pink eggs and guard them until they hatch. Meanwhile, the bright red and blue males wander about trying to impress the females. Although closely related to stink bugs, harlequin bugs don't squirt their enemies with bad odours. In a much more pleasant defence, they use their bright colours to warn predators that they taste awful.

Feather-legged bugs feed only on ants

Feather-legged assassin

Feather-legged bugs drug ants! There are about 10 species of these strange bugs living in Australia. All have fluffy hairs encircling the 'ankles' of the last pair of legs, which they wave around to attract the attention of ants. The ants are drawn to a gland on the bug's chest, which is thought to produce a secretion that drugs the ants, making them easy prey. Once captured, the ant is stabbed at the back of the head with the bug's rostrum and its body fluids are sucked out.

Cool summer choir

Cicadas have attracted a lot of attention over the years with their deafening summer chorus, their fascinating empty shells clinging to tree trunks and their amazing appearance! Cicadas spend their nymphal stage underground, feeding on the sap from plant roots. Some species spend one year in this stage; others up to ten. Adults – having shed their nymphal shell and spread their wings – live above ground, feeding on the same sap from tree stems. Females lay their eggs in slits in the branches and the tiny nymphs hatch out and drop to the ground to start the cycle again.

Know your cicadas

Years ago kids started making up common names for the different species of cicadas, and these have been passed down through the generations. Have you heard of the Black Prince, Floury Baker, Green Grocer, Masked Devil or Yellow Monday?

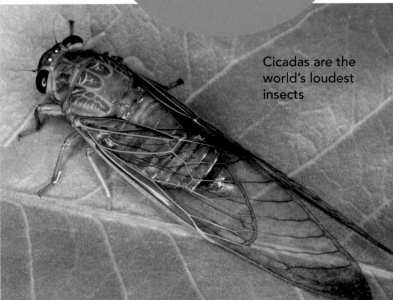

Cicadas are the world's loudest insects

Butterflies and Moths

Butterflies and moths are in the order Lepidoptera, meaning 'scaly wings'. The fine powder that gets on your fingers if you handle a butterfly or moth is actually scales. All species have a lifecycle where the egg hatches into a larva called a caterpillar, which looks very different to the adult insect and feeds very differently too. Caterpillars chew vegetation, while the adult butterflies and moths – if they feed at all – sip nectar from flowers.

A coat of many colours

All moths fly at night, right? Wrong! Not the Joseph's Coat Moth (*Agarista agricola*), which flies about by day. Judging by its bright colours (it's named after Joseph's coat of many colours) and slow flight it probably tastes awful. Its caterpillars feed on native relatives of grapes and are brightly banded in black white and orange, also colours that warn off predators.

Eastern Ringed Xenica Butterfly

Who is fluttering by?

So what's the difference between a butterfly and a moth? Not much! Generally speaking, butterflies have antennae with knobs on the end like little drumsticks; can fold their wings together over their backs while resting; flit around flowers by day; and pupate 'naked', without making a cocoon. Moths have antennae without knobs; rest with their wings flat; flap around lights at night; and spin cocoons to pupate. There are, of course, rare exceptions to these rules, with some twilight-flying butterflies and some moths with knobbed antennae!

Xenica butterflies

Xenica butterflies have caterpillars that eat grass. All three species are found in grassy areas. The caterpillars are well camouflaged and resemble the grasses they eat.

Ulysses Butterfly

Orchard Butterflies have taken to laying their eggs on introduced citrus plants, which are more abundant than the native citrus species

Ulysses Butterfly

One of the biggest butterflies in Australia, the Ulysses Butterfly is found in tropical Northern Queensland and Papua New Guinea. It lives in rainforests below the thick canopy. The caterpillar is green and white, to blend in with the plants it feeds on. The adult butterfly has beautiful metallic blue and black wings, with a wingspan of around 9 centimetres. In the hunt for a mate, Ulysses Butterflies are attracted to any blue object – natural or artificial – and can spot something blue 30 metres away!

Case moths

Case moths – known as bag worms in the USA – carry their homes with them. The caterpillars construct silken bags, strengthened with pieces of stick or leaf, which they carry with them as they travel and feed. This case becomes their cocoon when they pupate into moths. In most species, the adult moths don't feed and only the male has wings and leaves the case to mate. The female never leaves her case; mating through the end of it, laying her eggs inside and then dying. The tiny caterpillars hatch, then leave to spin their own cases.

A young Lewin's Case Moth

Rescuing the Richmond Birdwing

Sadly the Richmond Birdwing (*Ornithoptera richmondia*), one of our largest butterflies, was in danger of extinction. This was partly because its rainforest habitat was being destroyed, and also because it often mistakenly laid its eggs on an introduced species of plant that poisoned its caterpillars. Luckily people in north east NSW and south east Queensland began a campaign to save native bushland and plant native Aristolochia vines for the butterflies, whose numbers have increased as a result.

Centipedes and Millipedes

Centipedes rarely have 100 legs and millipedes never have 1000 legs! Millipedes range from having 50 to 350 pairs of legs, while centipedes range from 15 to 177 pairs. Centipedes (Myriopoda = 'many legs') and millipedes (Diplopoda = 'two legs') are two classes of arthropod invertebrates. Although similar in appearance, they are not very closely related and are easy to tell apart.

Mild-mannered millipedes

Millipedes have cylindrical bodies with a harder exoskeleton and two pairs of walking limbs per body segment (hence the class name Diplopoda). They have short, stiff, clubbed antennae and no venomous claws as they are mainly scavengers and detritovores, feeding on dead plant and animal matter and animal dung. Most millipedes coil up into a defensive spiral or roll into a ball when attacked.

Please wipe all your feet

Centipedes are generally flat, soft-bodied creatures, with long flexible antennae and only one pair of limbs per body segment. The last pair of walking legs is usually much longer than the front limbs, which are actually venom-injecting claws used in self-defence or to subdue prey. All centipedes are carnivorous and some of the larger species can catch and eat small snakes, lizards, even mice and bats. Centipedes keep themselves clean by running all of their many legs over their mouthpart to remove any dirt.

A large scolodrenpid centipede is powerful enough to catch lizards and small snakes

Nanny-hairy-legs

Nanny-hairy-legs, or house centipedes, are probably the best lost leg regrowers in the animal world. A scientist once discovered that one species could regrow all 30 legs back to their original size, without access to food, twice over. It's therefore hardly surprising to learn that dropping legs when threatened is a common way these centipedes escape predators. The dismembered limbs twitch and jiggle, distracting the enemy. House centipedes are one of the few species that venture inside houses, where they feed on silverfish, small cockroaches and other insects.

Long-legged centipedes, also known as nanny-hairy-legs, have compound eyes like an insect

Pill millipedes eat leaf litter

Pill millipede

Pill millipedes roll into a ball when threatened, making it hard for predators to reach their softer bellies or easily damaged legs. They are usually very shiny, which helps reduce friction as they bulldoze their way through soil and leaf litter. They feed on decaying leaves and twigs, fallen fruit and animal droppings. They do not eat living plants or animals. Newly hatched pill millipedes have fewer body segments and, therefore, fewer legs than their parents. As they grow, they shed their skins and add new segments and pairs of legs until they reach adult size. Some can reach the size of a marble when rolled up.

Cockatoos

Cockatoos are large parrots with gall bladders – which other parrots don't have! Cockatoos are mainly white, black or grey, often with patches of red, pink, orange or yellow, but never the blues and greens common in other parrots. All cockatoos have some sort of erectable crest on their head. They are noisy birds, which form large flocks and can be taught to mimic human words. They have been popular pets for centuries.

You great Galah

Galahs are a widely distributed species of pink and grey cockatoo. They feed on seeds of a variety of plants and grasses, which they usually eat from off the ground once the seeds have fallen. When a large flock is feeding, one Galah will keep its head up looking out for danger. Galahs are renowned for their often odd playful behaviour and a pair of Galahs will bond for life, capable of breeding for up to 40 years. They're found over much of Australia in timbered areas near water.

A Major Mitchell Cockatoo in flight

One tough bird

The Palm Cockatoo (*Probosciger aterrimus*) is a huge species of cockatoo with the strongest bite of any bird. It feeds on tough nuts and seeds from palm trees and other rainforest plants plus any wood boring grubs it can gouge out of tree branches. It is only found in Cape York in Australia, and in New Guinea. This unusual bird is a toolmaker and practises drumming! When a Palm Cockatoo wants to communicate with others of the species it breaks off a stick and beats it against a hollow trunk or on branches.

The Gang-gang gang

Gang-gang Cockatoos sound like squeaky gate hinges. They are usually found in alpine areas in small flocks, searching for seed pods, which they crack open for the seeds within. Male Gang-gangs have dark grey bodies with bright red heads, while the females are mottled grey all over.

Moving house

The old hollow trees the Long-billed Corella (*Cacatua tenoirostris*) needs to nest in are being removed from its south east Australian environment. It's not all bad news though, as this species can now be found living in other areas. Little Corellas (*Cacatua sanguinea*) are nomadic and very common in Australia. Also known as the Bare-eyed Corella, this cockatoo lives in flocks of thousands of birds. They roost in trees at night then leave in the morning to feed – can you imagine how loud thousands of screeching corellas would be! Little corellas have a distinctive blue-grey ring around their eyes.

Male Gang-gang Cockatoo develop red heads while females have grey heads

Short-billed or Little Corellas, like most cockatoos, are very acrobatic

Corals and other Cnidarians

Cnidarians are stingers! The phylum includes sea anemones, corals, jellyfish, sea-pens, hydroids and sea-wasps. 'Cnidaria' refers to the stinging organelles called cnidocysts that the group carries. They are simple animals that have a sac-like gut with the mouth also being the anus. A number of cnidarians have tiny single-cell algae called zooxanthellae living in their bodies, which provide them with oxygen and nourishment when exposed to sunlight.

Coral bleaching

Each coral usually contains only one species of zooxanthellae, which colours the coral, making the bright colours we see. When water gets too warm, great numbers of zooxanthellae are damaged by the heat and ejected by the coral, draining it not only of its vibrant colour, but also of essential nutrients. This is the cause of the coral bleaching that has been reported on the Great Barrier Reef.

Hard coral

Hard corals make coral islands, atolls and lagoons. They do this by absorbing calcium from the water to make a hard protective structure that they live in, and from which they can extend their tentacles at night to feed. Most coral species have evolved a symbiotic relationship with single-celled algae living in their tissues. The algae provide energy and help extract the calcium from the surrounding seawater when exposed to sunlight, so most corals are found in shallow warm water.

The colour in coral comes from the algae living inside it

Bluebottles are a common hazard on Australian beaches

The Waratah Anemone feeds on small rockpool animals

Nemo lives here

Anemones feed by fatally stinging their prey with their waving tentacles and pushing the food into their central mouth. This single opening means that any waste comes back out of the 'mouth' after digestion. Certain species of anemone have a special relationship with clownfish, made famous in the movie Finding Nemo. The clownfish is able to live amongst the anemone's stinging cells – lethal to most other fish – by secreting mucus, which covers their body and stops them from being zapped.

The nimble Jimble

Jimble jellyfish are not deadly – unlike their close relatives the box jellyfish and the Irukandji. These small, fast-swimming cubozoans can sting, but the result is usually treatable just by washing the wound with seawater or vinegar and removing any traces of tentacle. Jimbles hunt small fish and other tiny marine animals and are surprisingly nimble, usually able to avoid human swimmers by weaving around them. Jimbles are the most common type of box jellyfish in the southern half of Australia.

Irukandji

The Irukandji may be small, but it can be just as dangerous as its larger relative, the notorious box jellyfish. Irukandji (named after an Aboriginal tribe) are only about 2 cm across their cube-shaped body, with one long stinging tentacle hanging from each of the four corners. Humans have a strong reaction to the sting and they have caused a number of deaths. Being so small and almost transparent, Irukandji are hard to see in the water. They seem to have good vision and can avoid predators and obstacles, but they can be washed against people swimming.

Jimble jellyfish floating on the surface

Crocodiles

Crocodiles are the largest reptiles in the world, and the most ancient, dating back millions of years. All crocodiles are predators, feeding on aquatic creatures, birds, reptiles and mammals – even humans on occasion! Surprisingly crocodiles are very good parents and protect their eggs and young. Crocodiles are found in tropical Australia.

Friendly Freshies

The Freshwater, or Johnstone's, Crocodiles won't eat you. They have narrow jaws with long pointed teeth ideal for snatching fish out of the water or for impaling crustaceans, water insects and the occasional bird or small mammal. Large prey, up to the size of a wallaby, is occasionally taken, but Johnstone's Crocs prefer smaller prey as they are not good at tearing larger animals apart and generally try to swallow their dinner whole!

Scary Salties

Saltwater Crocodiles are the world's largest living reptiles. They can reach 7 metres in length and are powerful enough to prey upon cattle, horses and water buffalo. Usually, however, their prey consists of fish and turtles, waterbirds, reptiles (including Freshwater Crocodiles) and small mammals. Humans have been caught and eaten but, if given a choice, the crocodiles prefer other animals. Nevertheless, care should be taken if visiting wetlands in northern Australia.

Freshwater or Johnstone's Crocodile is found in northern Australian in freshwater rivers and billabongs. They can gallop to escape danger, which is a rare ability for a reptile

Large crocodiles can even catch water buffalo

Crikey!

Since the early 1970s crocodile hunting has been banned in Australia and the number of Saltwater Crocodiles has been increasing in some areas. As a result, many waterways in the tropics, which were formerly crocodile free, now have a resident croc due to habitat destruction and population pressures elsewhere. If considered a threat to people, these crocodiles are removed and taken to a more suitable location.

Saltwater Crocodiles must hide, or move, if their waterhole dries up

Crustaceans

Crustacea is a large class of arthropods, containing more than 50,000 species. Most species possess gills and a larval stage called a nauplius. Many also possess appendages that branch into two, for example claws, gills, swimming limbs and antennae. Most species are aquatic or amphibious, but some, such as slaters and woodlice, are wholly terrestrial. Many crustaceans are commercially important as food items for humans.

Garden slaters are good scavengers

Rose-coloured Barnacles are filter feeders

Barnacle hitchhikers

At first sight a barnacle looks more like some kind of mollusc than a crustacean. In its planktonic stage, the barnacle drifts around in the ocean currents. However, once it attaches itself headfirst to something to grow to adulthood, most species then have to stay put. Some species, however, fix themselves to floating planks of wood, pumice rocks and other things – even sea turtles! – and continue to drift about. Once fixed to a surface, barnacles extend their feathery limbs, or cirri, into the water to filter out any plankton to feed on.

Barnacle superglue

Have you ever tried to remove a barnacle from a rock? Their glue is amazingly strong and research is being done to discover the secrets of 'barnacle glue'. There's even talk of it being used by dentists to fit false teeth!

A spiny crayfish – these are prickly while yabbies are smooth

Is a yabby a crayfish?

No. Yabbies are smooth – crayfish are rough. That's the easiest way to tell them apart. Specifically the name 'yabby' should refer only to one species – *Cherax destructor* – but the name has been applied to relatives of this smooth-shelled crustacean, and often to the less closely related spiny crayfish as well. Yabbies are often found in stagnant farm dams or muddy rivers. They eat water plants, dead leaves and bark washed into the water, dead animals, or live ones – like water snails – too slow to move out of the way. The females carry their eggs and young beneath their tails.

Fine fiddlers

Fiddler crabs, also called caller crabs, belong to the genus *Uca*. The males have one tiny claw and one huge claw, which they wave about to attract the females, who have two normal-sized claws. They are found in holes in mangroves and mudflats where they emerge at low tide to feed on algae and detritus washed in by the tides and to court and battle amongst themselves. The tiny larval crabs drift out at sea for a short while before settling to the bottom and come ashore to live as an adult.

Isopods eat tongues

Isopods are small crustaceans related to prawns and lobsters. Most feed on decaying plant and animal material, but some known as 'fish lice' are parasites on fish. One type of fish louse lives in the mouth of the Leatherjacket and eats its tongue. It then takes the place of the tongue and even helps the fish to swallow like the real tongue, all the while feeding on the fish's blood!

A male Fiddler Crab has one big claw for courting

Cuckoos

Australian cuckoos are a mixed group in both size and way of life. Most, but not all, species do the famous cuckoo trick of laying their eggs in other birds' nests for them to raise, and none of them say 'cuck-oo', like the European ones which gave the group their name.

Big babysitters needed

Channelbill Cuckoos are the world's largest cuckoos which use other birds to raise their young. Being so large, Channelbills need large host birds, so use raven and crow, magpie and currawong nests. Adults migrate down from New Guinea and Indonesia to reach their Australian breeding grounds, where they call loudly during spring and summer. In late summer or early autumn they migrate back north, escaping the cold weather. Channelbills feed on fruit and insects, but also often eat the baby birds and eggs of their hosts!

Channelbill Cuckoos fly into Australia each year to breed

Pheasant Coucal

Also known as Swamp Pheasants these birds don't taste like pheasants and few animals bother eating them

Kooky-looking cuckoos

The Pheasant Coucal is the only Australian cuckoo species that raises its own chicks.
It would be hard to fool most other bird species that the peculiar coal black Coucal chicks, with the wispy white hair like feathers, were their own – maybe that's why coucals do the job themselves! Coucals are ground-dwelling birds and build their own nests hidden in thick grass or sugar cane.

Coo-ee ... it's going to rain

In Australia, perhaps the most well known cuckoo is the Koel, which gave us the famous Australian 'coo-ee' call. Koels are medium-sized cuckoos with black males and mottled brown females and young. They most often use Red-Wattle Honeyeaters and Pee Wees as host to raise their chicks. Koels have a reputation for predicting rain, and are sometimes called Rain Birds or Monsoon Birds. If you are familiar with their call, you will often notice it becomes more frequent and changes pitch as wet weather approaches.

Male Koels are black while female Koels are mottled brown like the youngsters

Female Koel

angerous Animals

Compared to other parts of the world Australia is virtually free of what are usually considered dangerous animals – lions, tigers, bears and the like. In the ten years, from 1980 to 1990, only 70 people were killed by wild animals. Nevertheless, there are many native Australian creatures that are potentially deadly if they are disturbed. In fact, Australia possibly has more venomous creatures than any other nation, in both the sea and on land, and some are quite surprising.

Deadly snail of the sea

Cone shells are molluscs, the marine relatives of garden snails. Unusually, they are voracious predators on other animals, from worms and other molluscs to small, fast-moving fish. Cones subdue their prey by 'harpooning' them, using a venomous barbed dart expelled from a very flexible proboscis, a bit like an elephant's trunk. The dart contains potent nerve venom, which rapidly paralyses the victim. Never pick up cone shells with bare hands, even if you think they're empty – people have died from their sting.

The Blue-ringed Octopus is one of the world's most dangerous octopuses.

Do not disturb

The Blue-ringed Octopus may be small, but it is the most dangerous octopus found in Australia. These tiny octopuses are shell-less molluscs and have very powerful venom mainly used for quickly dealing with its 'nippy' prey of crabs and other crustaceans, often as large as the octopus itself. It can also be deadly to humans. They can be found in shallow rock pools and when disturbed their bright blue rings and stripes are a clear warning to stay away.

Cone shells can catch and eat fish

Beware the barb

The huge Giant Black Stingray (*Dasyatis thetidis*) can grow up to 4 metres long and almost 2 metres wide. Despite recent reports of people being killed by stingray barbs such attacks are rare and occur only when a ray is accidentally stepped on, caught by anglers or otherwise threatened. Left alone they are harmless. However, they do have a sharp venomous spine that can pierce through a wetsuit or rubber-soled shoe. If the spine breaks off in the wound the ray can grow a new one.

Ducks

'Duck' is the common name for all members of the family Anatidae, which includes ducks, geese, teals and swans. All are waterbirds with webbed feet but the diet will vary slightly according to type of 'duck' and species. Some eat both plant and animal matter like tadpoles, water snails and water plants. Others such as geese feed primarily on grasses on land. Swans use their long necks to reach water plants growing on the bottom of the river bed.

Mixed-up ducks

One of the problems facing a number of native duck species is that they're too closely related to domestic farmyard ducks. This causes problems as escaped or dumped domestic ducks are more aggressive than the natives and will chase away the males and mate with the females, resulting in a mix of cross-breed ducks instead of the native species.

Black Ducks live in pairs or small flocks in all but the dryest areas of Australia

Chestnut Teal

Chestnut Teal

Chestnut Teal (*Anas castanea*) don't mind the salt. Although they can be found in coastal freshwater areas and swamps they are equally happy in saltwater rivers and estuaries as long as they can get access to fresh water to drink. Chestnut Teal eat seeds, water plants and small animals in the shallow water and mud where they can collect them by tipping head down/bottom up in the shallows – a process known as dabbling.

Wood Ducks eat grass

Wood Duck

Wood Ducks are actually more closely related to geese than they are to true ducks – they are sometimes known as Maned Geese. They feed mainly on land grasses, but will also eat reeds and other aquatic vegetation. Wood Ducks nest in hollow branches and trees, rather than on the ground like most other Ducks and geese. This gives them protection while incubating the eggs, but it means the tiny ducklings must jump to the ground from quite a height and then scurry after their mother for some distance to reach the safety of the water.

Echinoderms

Echinodermata means 'spiny skin' and is the phylum name for starfish, sea cucumbers, sea urchins and sea lilies. They are unusual animals with members who can regenerate from a single 'leg'; can regurgitate their digestive tract to distract predators or digest food; and have water, rather than blood, pumped through their circulatory system. They are also radially symmetrical, which means if you were to slice them in half from top to bottom, each half would be a mirror image of the other half.

The Slate Pencil Urchin feeds on algae

Slate Pencil Urchin

The thick stubby spines on a Slate Pencil Urchin (*Phyllacanthus parvispinus*) are used to wedge the animal into rock crevices where the waves can't wash it back out. The mouth of sea urchins faces the bottom while their anus is at the top of their round bodies. This is useful to them as they mostly graze on algae growing on the rocks they crawl over. For this reason they appear to us to be walking about upside-down! Slate Pencil Urchins get their common name from the spines resembling pencils used to mark the old writing slates used by schoolchildren in bygone days before the 'modern' graphite and paper class rooms. When they die the shell of a sea urchin remains after the soft tissue inside has rotted away and the spines have fallen out. These empty shells are called tests and are sometimes washed up onto beaches.

Crown-of-thorns Starfish

At a diameter of 40 centimetres, covered in venomous spines, the Crown-of-thorns is the world's biggest and most dangerous starfish. It was once considered a rare species and little was known about it, so when stories of outbreaks of these huge starfish swarming over and devouring the coral reefs first appeared it was hard to believe. The cause of these outbreaks is still not fully known. Nutrient-rich soil run-off from farms creates excellent conditions for the starfish, but research shows that similar 'plagues' of Crown-of-thorns Starfish have occurred many times over the centuries.

Crown-of-thorns Starfish can cause painful stings as well

Commercial cucumbers

Sea cucumbers, dried and sold as Bêche-de-mer or Trepang, has been a popular Asian delicacy for centuries. It is also known as Gamat in some countries, and thought to have special healing properties.

Sea Cucumber

Sea cucumbers can regurgitate part of their respiratory organs if threatened. This will either distract or deter many predators as the contents taste awful! Sea cucumbers eat plankton and detritus sucked up from the seabed, or filtered from the water. A lot of fine, inedible rubble is also taken in this way and their guts are often full of sand. Quite bizarrely, the Pearlfish makes its home inside the sea cucumber, entering tail-first through its bottom and only coming out at night to feed!

Which end is which? Sea cucumbers actually breathe through their bottoms!

Flightless Birds

There are four species of flightless birds commonly found in Australia, and two of the largest birds in the world! Emus and cassowaries belong to the ratite group of birds (order Struthioniformes), which also includes the Ostrich, kiwis and the extinct moas of New Zealand. The Little Penguin, or Fairy Penguin, is the only penguin species to nest on the Australian mainland and offshore islands. The Tasmanian Native Hen is a member of the rail family, whose relatives can all fly quite well.

The littlest penguin

Also known as the Fairy Penguin, this is the smallest penguin species in the world. Standing only 45 centimetres tall, these cute little birds 'fly' under water using their wings like flippers. They can remain under water for at least a minute, while pursuing their prey. At dusk, the penguins gather in groups called 'rafts' just offshore and then waddle back to their burrows after sunset. After the breeding season, the adults moult and must remain ashore until their feathers have regrown.

Fairy Penguins breed in burrows on the shore

Tasmanian Native Hen

Tasmanian Native Hen

These birds are flightless grass-eating relatives of coots and moorhens and are now found only in Tasmania. The Tasmanian Native Hen is quite a large bird and forms family groups or clans that defend an area of grassy land near watercourses against other clans of native hens. Interestingly, it seems to have benefited from European settlement and has increased in number, as land clearing and even the introduced rabbits and cattle create the shorter grass and cleared areas it likes.

Cassowary

The cassowary is Australia's second largest native bird – and the third largest bird in the world – reaching 1.8 metres in height. Cassowaries look like they're covered in black, bristly hair, but these are actually tough modified feathers, allowing cassowaries to crash through often thorny vegetation in their rainforest homes. Adults have bony head crests called casques, and blue and red naked heads and necks. Southern Cassowaries feed mainly on fallen fruits, helping spread the seeds of rainforest trees.

Emus are found in woodland and other habitats throughout much of Australia

Extraordinary Emu eggs

Emus are the second largest birds in the world – only a little smaller than ostriches. Emus are unusual in that the males do all the brooding of the eggs and then raise the striped chicks, while the females may go off and lay eggs in other males' nests. Their beautiful big green eggs are very popular with artists, who carve pictures into the shell. Carving through the layers of the shell reveals different shades of colour. Because Emus are protected, you need to be registered and licensed to sell or collect eggs.

Southern Cassowaries have a dangerous kick if threatened

Freshwater Fishes

Compared to other parts of the world, Australia has relatively little diversity and few species of freshwater fishes, most of which are closely related to their marine ancestors. Some species spend most of their lives in fresh water, then leave to spawn in the ocean. Others, spend most of their lives in the ocean, but enter fresh water to spawn. Some of our freshwater fish fauna is quite distinct and of great scientific interest; while others have unusual behaviour or are important as target species for recreational anglers.

Fish or fishes?

The plural of one species of fish is 'fish' (for example a school of Globe Porcupine Fish), while the plural of more than one species of fish is 'fishes' (for example, a mixed school of fishes including Globe Porcupine Fish, Blue Mackeral and Nepean Herring).

Cod in captivity

Murray Cod are Australia's largest freshwater fish, reaching lengths of almost 2 metres, although wild specimens of 70 cm are considered large these days. They are large-mouthed fish that can swallow other fishes and yabbies, as well as water insects and other invertebrates. Many freshwater cod species have declined or disappeared due to pressures like river pollution, introduced fishes, removal of snags and fallen timber in the rivers and overfishing. Murray Cod are now being bred in captivity and restocked in much of their former range.

Murray Cod are Australia's largest freshwater fish

Bullrouts are freshwater relatives of the stonefishes

Don't step on a bullrout

Bullrouts are small freshwater relatives of stonefish – and like them have good camouflage and venomous spines that dish out an excruciating sting. Bullrouts are thought to breed in estuaries, yet they have also been caught in freshwater habitats with no connection to the sea. In fact, little is known about their habits and breeding. Bullrouts grow to up to 30 centimetres and feed on small fish, shrimp and aquatic insects, which they ambush when the prey wanders too close. Beware where you step in the coastal streams along eastern Australia!

Like a fish out of water

Lungfishes first appeared in the fossil record 380 million years ago. Australian Lungfish are the most primitive in the world, having only one lung and able to survive only a few days out of water. Other species have two lungs and can survive without water for months. Australian lungfish can grow to 1.5 metres long, and the oldest known fish in captivity is an 80-year-old lungfish. They lay eggs like a frog's and the young lungfish have external gills similar to some tadpoles.

Water-pistol fish

Archerfish, also called riflefish, 'shoot' prey with 'arrows' or 'bullets' of water. They inhabit rivers and estuaries in northern Australia, cruising below the surface until they see an insect on plants overhead. Getting closer, they tilt up and spit a series of high-pressure water drops, knocking the unfortunate insect off its perch into the water where it's rapidly swallowed before another fish steals it. Archerfish have been known to extinguish people's cigarettes on riverbanks at night, mistaking them for fireflies!

The Queensland Lungfish is the only lungfish in the world that can't survive for long periods out of water – despite its lung!

Frogs

Frogs are the only native amphibians found in Australia. We have one introduced salamander – the Mexican Axolotl, available only from pet shops – and one introduced toad – the Cane Toad, whose introduction was a disastrous attempt at a biological control of two native sugar-cane beetle pests. Australia does, however, have a great diversity of more than 200 species of frogs in four families, most being found nowhere else in the world.

Pesty toads

Cane Toads are the only true toads in Australia. They were introduced in 1935 to help control beetles that were attacking sugar cane crops. Big mistake! These large, warty amphibians eat just about anything, grow very quickly and are poisonous. They are now considered a pest as they compete with native animals for food and animals die after eating them because of their poison.

The Ornate Nursery Frog is a tiny rainforest frog that makes a big 'beep' noise

Nursery Frog

These tiny frogs in northern Australia lay eggs that hatch directly into even tinier frogs, without an independent tadpole stage! Through the clear jelly coating of the eggs you can watch the tadpoles growing their legs and absorbing their tails, all within the confines of the eggshell. The name 'Nursery Frog' comes from the behaviour of the males, who stay close to the eggs, protecting them from both predators and disease. For their size, they have surprisingly loud voices, giving various species names like 'Buzzing Frog' and 'Cricket Chirpers'.

Sphagnum Frog

Sphagnum Frogs (*Philoria sphagnicola*) can vary in colour and can be any shade from black to cream or red to yellow. As their name suggests they are often found in sphagnum or peat bogs in alpine areas in Australia. They can also be found in other damp mountain habitats like Antarctic Beech Forests where they live in tunnels dug under rotted logs or rocks. Like its close relative, the Baw Baw Frog, it lays eggs that hatch into non-feeding tadpoles, which then change into tiny frogs.

Sphagnum Frogs are small ground-dwelling frogs that eat ants and other insects

Crucifix Frog

This is one of four known species in the genus *Notaden*. All feed primarily on ants and have brightly coloured bodies or patterns to advertise that they taste yucky! The Crucifix Frog has a cross pattern on its yellow back made up of black, red and white warts, which produce a nasty taste. Most of its life is spent buried underground near arid clay pans. When rains flood the clay pans, the moisture soaks down to the buried frogs and they emerge to feast and breed.

Crucifix Frogs are found in central NSW and Queensland and feed mainly on small black ants

One sticky trick

One species of *Notaden* frog is nicknamed the 'Superglue Frog'. It produces a gummy skin secretion, which glues up the mouth of any animal that tries to eat it.

Eastern Pobblebonks are sometimes called Banjo Frogs

Pobblebonk frogs

This name is given to several burrowing frogs that all make a 'bonk' call like a banjo. When one male frog calls, any others close by call back and the result is a rapid series of calls that sound like 'pobblebonk'! Pobblebonks call from the edges of billabongs, waterholes or farm dams, usually at night, from concealed positions in the bank. They have poison glands on their back legs specifically to discourage snakes from eating them, as snakes tend to swallow frogs back legs first.

Why are frogs disappearing?

Why are frog and other amphibian numbers around the world declining? The answer is we don't know for sure but it seems to be happening all around the world at the same time. Many suggestions or causes are known like disease and habitat destruction but the only one which seems to fit the global decline is climate change, which frogs are very vulnerable to. Changes to temperature and environment are likely to make other problems worse and so frogs might be dying from diseases brought on by climate-change stresses.

Baw Baw Frog

Baw Baw frogs are very rare and restricted in distribution, found only in parts of the Mount Baw Baw Plateau in eastern Victoria. They have unusual tadpoles that are creamy white on hatching and don't feed until they become tiny frogs. Baw Baws require cool climates and populations have declined in recent years for a number of reasons, including habitat destruction, disease, introduced predators, and now probably climate change.

Gliders

Gliders are the marsupial equivalent of 'flying squirrels'. These active possums can glide from tree to tree, using flaps of skin stretching from wrists to ankles. This means they can largely avoid ground-dwelling predators. The Greater Glider is the largest species and is about the size of a cat. The tiny Feather-tailed Glider is the smallest and is only the size of a mouse.

Greater Gliders

The Greater Glider (*Petauroides volans*) is the largest gliding marsupial in the world. It is also the gliding possum with the most restrictive diet as it is a leaf-eater, feeding mainly on eucalypt leaves and buds. Also, unlike the other gliding possums which have the gliding membrane (those flaps of skin which allow them to glide) stretching between wrist and ankle, those of the Greater Glider run from the elbow to the ankle, making them resemble a frying pan when gliding. As these are large animals they are usually found in the tall trees of cool mountain forests with lots of hollows for them to rest in during the day.

Greater Gliders are cat-sized but much lighter

Yellow-bellied Glider

These large gliders eat sap from eucalypt trees. They make strange herring-bone patterned gouges in the bark to make the sap flow. These patterns are often the only visible sign of the gliders during the day – however, they can often be seen returning to the same tree gouges each night to reopen their sap grooves and feed. Yellow-bellied Gliders are one of the noisiest mammals in the Australian bushland. They communicate with each other in a series of shrieks and gurgles, which can make for an eerie night's camping!

Yellow-bellied Gliders love eating the sap from some trees. They are also the best at gliding of all the gliding possums

Leadbeater's Possums are quite rare

Leadbeater's Possum

Leadbeater's Possum (*Gymnobelidius leadbeateri*) is most likely very similar to the ancestor of most species of Australian glider. The resemblance of these small possums to their relatives, the Sugar, Squirrel and Yellow-bellied Gliders is obvious, even though they don't possess a gliding membrane themselves. Interestingly, Leadbeater's Possum is one of the mammals that depends on fire for its survival, as it requires a mixture of recent regrowth, Acacias, and hollows and branches in trees for its survival. Fires tend to provide this sort of pattern in the mountain ash forests where it lives. The trees require fires to set seed, but the fires themselves may kill off the 120-year-old trees that contain the hollows, so a particular regime of low level and infrequent fires are needed to help the Leadbeater's Possum survive.

# nsects

Insects are a class of the phylum Arthropoda. They have three pairs of jointed legs, plus three body parts – head, thorax and abdomen. Many of the insect orders contain winged species and were certainly the first animal group ever to take to the air, having been on Earth since way before the time of the dinosaurs. Their ability to fly has enabled them to colonise every continent in the world, except Antarctica, and their incredible diversity means that they affect almost all other land-based flora and fauna.

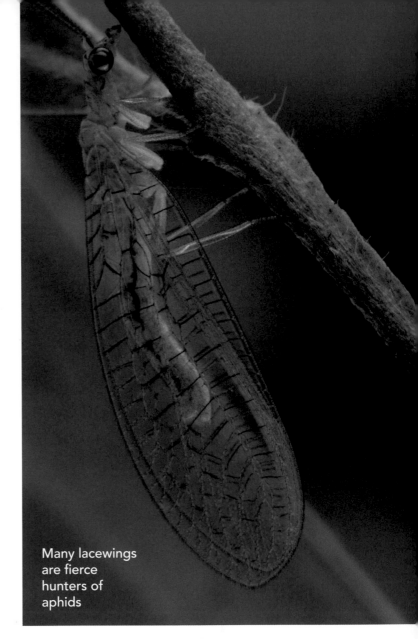

Many lacewings are fierce hunters of aphids

Lacewings in disguise

Lacewings may look delicate, but they are ferocious predators. Have you ever seen a batch of tiny white eggs each mounted on a short threadlike stalk which is attached to a leaf, tree or even the window sill? These are lacewing eggs and the larvae that hatch out have curved pincer-like jaws. They feed on other tiny insects and many species disguise themselves by putting the dried remains of their dinner onto their backs!.

Katydids are called bush crickets in Europe

How hot is it, Hoppy?

Did you know that grasshoppers can tell you the temperature? It's true! Being cold-blooded, their level of activity depends on the outside temperature – so the warmer it is the faster they can move or sing. For some species, if you count the number of chirps per minute and then use a mathematical equation, you will get the correct temperature. The problem is, each species calls at a different rate, so the equation is different for each species.

Listen to the music

Katydids are a type of grasshopper with long antennae They eat a range of food according to their species: some are entirely vegetarian; others entirely carnivorous; yet others are omnivorous, feeding on both plants and small animals. Most male katydids 'sing' by rubbing a 'file' on the left wing with a 'scraper' on the right, to produce a variety of sounds. In order to hear these sounds, katydids have an ear on each front leg, just below their knees!

Insects

An indigestible diet

Termites are highly social insects and although sometimes known as 'white ants', they belong to a completely different order (Isoptera) closely related to cockroaches. They are the only social insects that have sterile workers of both sexes (ant, bee and wasp workers are all females) and fertile males, which have a similar lifespan to the fertile females. They also have a symbiotic relationship with protozoa living in their gut, which help to break down their relatively indigestible wood and cellulose diet into something they can digest.

Upside-down flies

Upside-down flies are a small group of flies, discovered in 1978, that seem to do everything upside down! They even walk upside down, and if they need to go sideways, they will often follow a zig-zag course so they can keep their head down. The larvae (maggots) feed on micro-organisms in the fluid around the base of a flower or within the bracts of large-leafed plants, but the adults seem to feed on pollen.

'Magnetic' termites have their mounds pointing north-south to help with temperature control.

Wasps without wings

Velvet 'ants' are actually wingless female flower wasps. They are covered in fine hairs, giving them a velvety appearance. When ready to mate, the female wasps give off a scent that the larger, winged males find irresistible. The male zooms down, collects the female and together they fly off to visit the flowers that the female could never reach on her own. Sometimes the male feeds the female by mouth, which looks like 'kissing'! After mating, the male drops her and she looks for beetle larvae, which she paralyses with her sting, and lays her eggs on. When the eggs hatch, the wasp larvae feed on the paralysed host insect.

Only male velvet ants have wings

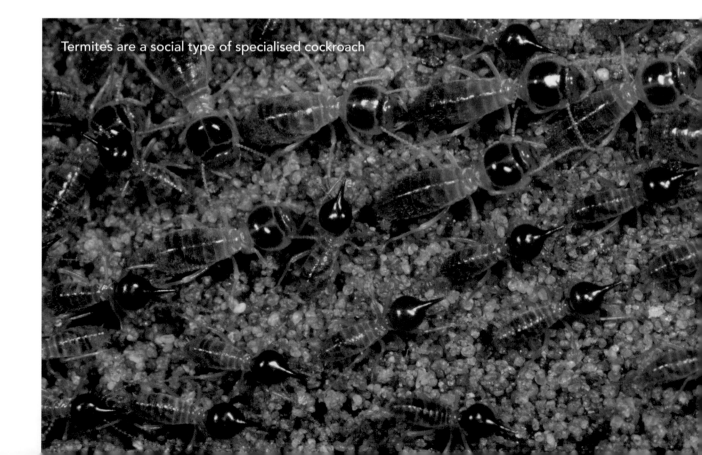

Termites are a social type of specialised cockroach

Kangaroos and Wallabies

Kangaroos are the largest living marsupials. Although the kangaroo family (Macropodidae) contains animals ranging in size from a large rabbit to species taller than an average human, the name is generally restricted to the five largest species: Red Kangaroos, Eastern Grey Kangaroos, Western Grey Kangaroos (including the Kangaroo Island Kangaroo), Antilopine Kangaroos and Hill Kangaroos (or Wallaroos). Wallabies are just a small type of kangaroo, however some are different enough to be given their own genus.

Red Kangaroos are fond of fresh green grasses and herbs

Big red boomer

The Red Kangaroo is the largest marsupial in the world – males can reach a height of 1.8 metres. It is usually the males that are red, while the females are a blue/grey colour. Red Kangaroos are nomads and will travel considerable distances to areas where there has been recent rainfall, so they can gorge on the fresh new grass. Their hopping gait expends very little energy, so they can travel many kilometres in a night, covering more than 9 metres in a single leap.

Quokkas of Rat Nest Island

The first people to see Quokkas – a type of small wallaby – were Dutch sailors, who thought they were large rats and named the island they found them on Rottnest (rat nest) Island! Quokkas are restricted to Rottnest Island and parts of the nearby mainland around Perth in Western Australia. Living in such dry areas, they get most of the moisture they need from the grasses and leaves they eat. They have no close relatives amongst the kangaroo family, being the sole member of the *Setonix* genus.

Tree kangaroos

Australia has two species of tree kangaroo – Bennett's and Lumholtz's – each named after early naturalists. Tree kangaroos are found in the tropical rainforests of Queensland, where they really do live in trees. They have powerful front legs with razor sharp claws and short back feet with rough soles to help with climbing. They are far less agile in the trees than possums and if threatened, they will often leap straight out of the tree and take their chances hopping away on the ground. They were a popular food item with Indigenous peoples, but are also eaten by eagles and pythons.

Lumholtz's Tree Kangaroo can jump from great heights

Hare-wallaby today, gone tomorrow

When Europeans first arrived in Australia there were five living species of hare-wallaby – now there are only three, two of which are endangered. Hare-wallabies are named after their resemblance to European hares in both size and speed. Unfortunately they are prey for feral cats and foxes, but luckily populations of all the surviving hare-wallaby species have been found on predator-free offshore islands in Western Australia.

Banded Hare Wallaby are very fast

Koalas and Wombats

Australia is famous for its amazing array of interesting animals, and many of our most well-loved icons – kangaroos, Koalas, wombats and numbats – are marsupials. Marsupials produce tiny underdeveloped young after a very short gestation period, which are then nurtured in a pouch, or marsupium, before they become independent.

Tree-climbing wombats?

Koalas are famous for a number of reasons: they rarely drink, obtaining almost all the moisture they need from their diet of gum leaves; they have 'thumbs', which gives them a firmer grip in the trees; and thirdly, they're just so cute! Koalas could be described as tree-climbing wombats. Because wombats burrow into the ground, their pouch opening faces backwards so it won't fill with earth during digging. The Koala also has this rear-opening pouch, though it might be considered a disadvantage sitting high up in the trees!

Burrow party by invitation only

There are three species of wombat in Australia today. All live in burrows and emerge at night to feed. The Common Wombat leads a solitary life in its own burrow, whereas the Southern and Northern Hairy-nosed Wombats are more social and can have elaborate warren systems, sometimes connecting several individual burrows. Wombats are fairly docile, but they can charge, bite and scratch very effectively if provoked. If any unwanted visitors stray into the burrows, wombats will crush them against the burrow walls.

Hairy-nosed Wombats inhabit more arid areas than Common Wombats

Save our koalas

Koalas are becoming very rare in some areas and increasing in number in other areas, for a variety of reasons. Habitat loss, road fatalities, bushfires and feral dogs claim many lives. But in other areas, a lack of natural predators and 'islands' of bushland surrounded by inhospitable cleared land or ocean can result in populations outgrowing the available food supply. In such cases, starvation may kill off hundreds of Koalas, as occurred in the past on Kangaroo Island.

Koalas have two opposable fingers on their hands giving them two thumbs and a strong grip

Lizards

Australia has more species of lizard than any other country. There are five families of lizards represented here: goannas, skinks, geckoes, legless lizards and dragons. They range in length from a few centimetres to over 2 metres and feed on a variety of foods according to their species. Although some could give you a painful bite if threatened, none are dangerous to humans and all perform a beneficial role in keeping down insect pests, eating carrion or providing food for other animals.

Go, go, goanna!

Goannas, also called monitor lizards, are Australia's largest lizards – although not all goannas are big. The tiny Short-tailed Goanna is the world's smallest species of this family, being only 25 centimetres long, compared to the Perentie, which can reach 2 metres. All goannas are predatory, eating a range of invertebrates, small mammals, other reptiles, bird eggs and even carrion. As well as being a traditional food source for the Aboriginal people, the goanna is a symbol of strength and power featuring in many stories from the Dreaming.

Dragons and devils

Australian dragons are all egg layers and all feed on smaller animals, although many species also eat some plant matter. The very spiky, fierce-looking Thorny Devil is in the dragon family and is actually quite harmless. It feeds almost exclusively on small black ants, eating up to 3000 ants one at a time in a single meal! Dragons come from a variety of habitats and can be found almost anywhere in Australia. They range in size from less than 10 centimetres to almost a metre.

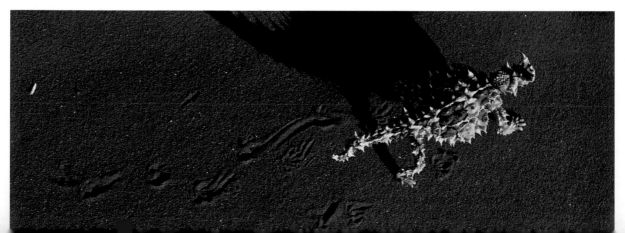

Eastern Water Dragons often take up residence in suburban gardens like this young male

Eastern Water Dragon

Eastern Water Dragons are Australia's largest dragon lizard and reach almost a meter in length. They are quite common around some suburban areas and parks and readily become tame in places where they are fed or left alone. Like many dragons when alarmed they may run away on their back legs only before dropping down on all fours when a safe distance away. They may also climb trees to escape predators or dive into water where they can swim very well and hide on the bottom. Males have a red chest while females and young are mainly brown.

The thrilling Frilled-neck

The Frilled-neck Lizard is one of the most spectacular dragon lizards. It has a broad flap of skin around its neck, which it can erect like an umbrella to frighten predators and rivals alike. If the frill display doesn't work, the lizard can also speedily run away and can swiftly climb trees too. However, the display isn't all bluff – the Frilled-neck has a powerful bite for its size, should all other defences fail.

Blue-tongued Lizard

Blue-tongued Lizards (*Tiliqua* species) are found everywhere in Australia except southwest Tasmania. All five Australian species are stocky, short-legged lizards of the family Scincidae with a prominent blue tongue. All give birth to live young rather than eggs. Their diet includes insects, snails, and plants and fungi. For some reason they are fond of yellow-coloured flowers if they can reach them. Blue-tongues are closely related to the Shingleback Lizards.

Sand swimmers

Sand swimmers are a group of burrowing skink lizards, which, when threatened, appear to swim into loose sand or soil to escape. They all posses smooth shiny scales, which allow them to slip easily through the earth. Many of them have reduced numbers of toes – or sometimes even a few missing limbs – as they are of little use to these eel-like burrowers. Most species feed on small insects and their larvae.

Narrow-banded Sand Swimmers can swim through loose sand

Perentie power

The Perentie, Australia's largest lizard, is found in central Australia. It will feed on any animal it can overpower – up to the size of a half-grown kangaroo, if it can catch one – and can easily deal with the most venomous snakes in the area. The Perentie happily devours carrion, although it is in danger of being hit by a car itself, when scavenging by the side of the road. Some goannas lay eggs in termite mounds, where the constant activity of the insects keeps the eggs warm. However, Perenties lays eggs under large rock outcrops.

Perenties can swallow dangerous snakes with no ill effects

Shinglebacks pair for life

Shingleback

This strange-looking lizard's head and tail look the same, so when threatened they curl up with the head and tail side-by-side, confusing predators into making a grab for the wrong end! They are mainly vegetarian, but will also eat any small animal that is too slow to get out of their way – and that's pretty slow! Shinglebacks, who pair for life, are not prolific breeders, like their coastal blue-tongued relatives, producing one to three live young, rather than eggs.

M ammals

Australia has more diversity and subclasses of mammals than anywhere else in the world. We have two species of monotreme, about 157 species of marsupial and around 155 species of placental mammals. In order to qualify as a mammal, an animal must have the following features: hair somewhere on the body; warm blood (homeothermy); and feed its young on milk. Almost all mammals give birth to live young, except monotremes, which lay eggs. The placentals, including humans, give birth to comparatively well-developed young.

Tasty termites for dinner again

Numbats are one of only two Australian land mammals active mainly by day (diurnal). These stripy little marsupials have a bushy tail, which they carry erect as they move, and feed almost exclusively on termites. Once common over most of southern Australia, it is now found only in a few spots in Western Australia. This decline is almost certainly due to the introduction of the Red Fox. The Numbat's survival has been largely thanks to the indigenous *Oxylobium* plant (Poison Peas), which produces a natural poison that is fatal to foxes when they eat animals that have eaten it – like Woylies, which live in the same areas as the Numbats.

Numbats are active termite eaters

Dugongs feed on
sea grasses

Sea cow or mermaid?

Dugongs are marine mammals sometimes called 'sea cows' and – as you might expect – they eat sea grass. They belong to a very small order of mammals, order Sirenia, which includes the similar Manatees of the Americas. Dugongs often raise their heads from the water to breathe or look around and they sometimes suckle their young in this upright position, appearing almost human. It is thought this may have inspired the mermaid legends – but you'd need a great imagination to mistake a 400-kilogram blubbery dugong with a whiskery chin for a beautiful maiden with a tail!

Dingo

The Dingo is regarded by some people as a native animal, because it was here before European settlement, and by others as a feral animal brought by Indigenous Australians and traders from South East Asia. It is descended from the Asiatic Wolf, but in recent years has often been crossed with domestic dogs, so many Dingoes are not pure-breds. Dingoes are placental animals like us and, like most of the dog family, they feed on meat and bones, either hunting live prey or scavenging carrion.

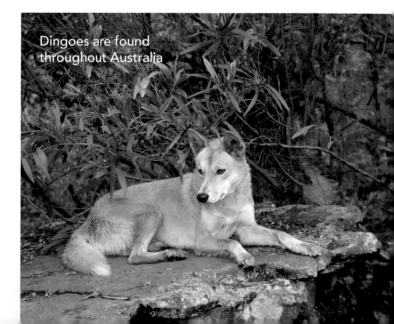

Dingoes are found throughout Australia

Marine Fishes

Fish breathe water. They are the only group (Class Pisces) of vertebrates that all have gills throughout their life and primarily breathe water. Australian marine fishes are very diverse. We have species that live in deep water, shallow water and just below the surface; species found in very few localities, those found in oceans around the world and species from all three major fish subclasses. The diverse fish fauna of the tropics, especially the Great Barrier Reef, is world famous.

Seriously slimy hagfish

Hagfish are the best slime producers of the seven seas! They have a number of common names – slime-eels, slime-hags and hag-eels – none of them nice. Hagfish are jawless, deepwater fish, feeding on dead or dying animals (they can strip a whale carcass to the bone) and making themselves unpopular with deep-sea fishermen by boring their way into hooked fishes and eating them alive from the inside out. They also enter crab and lobster traps and exude so much slime that they suffocate the catch and render the pots unusable until cleaned.

Gone fishing

An 'angler' is a fisherman; an anglerfish goes fishing for other fish! There are many anglerfish species. Deepwater species use a long spine on their dorsal fin with a glowing-tipped lure. Shallow water species have an extraordinary appendage that looks like a line and bait on their head. The shape of the bait in different species resembles the prey's favourite food, such as a worm, crustacean or fish, which is dangled in front of the anglerfish's mouth. When the prey gets close enough – gulp! – it's swallowed whole.

Anglerfish fish for other fishes!

The spikey Fortescue

Fortescue are small freshwater and brackish water relatives of the stonefishes. They can give a very painful but not fatal sting with their dorsal fin spines if stepped on. They are predators that ambush passing prey of small fish and shrimps.

Fortescue are a painful nuisance to prawn netters

Dazzling Dolphinfish

Unlike dolphins, Dolphinfish are true fish, not mammals. They are among the fastest of the ocean fishes in order to match their fast-moving prey, which includes the flying fishes and squids. They are also among the most colourful, dazzling with iridescent blues, greens, gold and orange. Dolphinfish are a popular food source, sold as Mahi Mahi or Dorado, but unfortunately their dazzling colours quickly fade after death.

Fish that walk

Mudskippers are fish that live on land. They use their fins like legs to walk or use their tails to hop across the mud. There are four main types of mudskipper: mud hoppers, mudsliders, the more typical mudskippers, and the huge King mudskipper, which prowls the river's edges ready to pounce on small crabs and fish! All can breathe air either through their wet skin, the lining of their throat and mouth, or in spongy gill membranes.

Mudskippers are the most nimble fish on land and can even climb trees

Marine Fishes

Sawtail surgeonfish have sharp cutting blades in their tail but mainly feed on algae

Saw-tailed Surgeonfish

Surgeonfishes (*Prionurus microlepidotus*) get their name from sharp knife like scutes (horny or bony plates on the body) on either side of their tails – they can use these to slash at other fish if they are attacked. In some species there may only be a single blade on each side of the body but in others – like the Sawtail Surgeonfish there can be a number on each side. Surgeonfish are mainly vegetarian and scrape seaweed off rocks and coral. Baby Sawtail Surgeonfish are brownish with yellow tails.

Zebra Lionfish are sometimes called Turkey Cod

Zebra Lionfish

Zebra Lionfish can sting you if you're not careful. Their bold-striped colouration is a warning to predators – and clumsy humans – to stay away. The sting is delivered by a series of venomous dorsal fin spines, much like its relatives, the stonefishes. The Zebra Lionfish is a predator of small fishes and shrimp. Its pretty pectoral fins are used to herd small fishes into dead-end nooks and crannies in the rocks. Once trapped the prey is swallowed with a lightning- fast snap of the jaws.

Queensland Grouper

The Queensland Grouper, or Giant Grouper, is the largest fish with a bony skeleton you will find on a coral reef. It can reach almost three metres in length and weigh up to 600 kilograms. Groupers are harmless to humans and are often sought out by divers for photo opportunities. The feeling seems to be mutual, as they will come out of their coral caves to observe divers, sometimes swimming with them over some distance. Queensland Groupers also change sex – starting off as female and becoming male when they reach a certain size.

Groupers have huge mouths but are generally harmless to humans

Zebrafish

Zebrafish are also known as Stripy Bream and are only found in Australian waters. They are not to be confused with the freshwater Zebrafish, or Zebra Danio, which is not a native species. Zebrafish are schooling fish which reach about 50 centimetres in length but have rather small mouths for their size. They are found around the southern coastal half of Australia – usually in the shallower rocky areas and their sharp teeth allow them to graze on algae and other seaweeds around the rock surfaces. Zebrafish are shy fish and hard to approach underwater.

Zebrafish are easily recognised

Megapodes

Megapodes are also known as incubator birds or mound nesters. They are an unusual group that has abandoned making nests, brooding and raising their young. Instead they rake together large mounds of rotting vegetation and earth and allow the warmth from decomposition to incubate the eggs. Australia has three species of megapodes: the Junglefowl, the Brush Turkey and the Mallee Fowl.

Malleefowl

The Malleefowl, found in the mallee belt across much of southern Australia, is the most southerly living Megapode species in the world. The Malleefowl is unusual in that it inhabits arid lands, while its relatives live in the more humid tropics. The drier country should make vegetation decompose more slowly in its mound, but the birds' careful mound tending ensures that the eggs are incubated at the right temperature. Although large and solid, Malleefowl can be very hard to see as they freeze when alarmed, before flying to cover if the danger gets too close.

Malleefowl, like all megapodes, don't care for their young after they hatch

Feathered thermometers

Once the female Junglefowl, or Brush Turkey, has laid her eggs, it's the male's job to keep the temperature of the mound at the correct level for the eggs to hatch. Throughout the day he will dig a small hole in the mound and insert his head. If it is too warm he will scrape off some of the litter and sand from the top of the mound. If it is too cold he will add more. After the chicks hatch, there is no further parental care and the chicks must fend for themselves.

Orange-footed Scrubfowl or Junglefowl may build the largest nests of all Australian Megapodes

Volcanic incubators

Some megapode species from South East Asia go one step further and bury their eggs in the ground kept permanently warm around volcanic vents!

Brush Turkeys are our most colourful megapodes

Molluscs

Despite often being called shellfish, many molluscs are shell-less. The phylum Mollusca is very diverse and includes octopus, squid, nautilus, snails, slugs, oysters, clams, pipis and nudibranchs. The features they all have in common are: a soft unsegmented body with a glandular slippery skin; a muscular 'foot', multiple 'arms', or a tongue-like structure; and a mantle – which can secrete a shell if the mollusc needs one.

Limpets can wear cavities in rocks after years of use

Scrolled snail shells

Volutes are a family of predatory marine snails prized for their attractive shells. The shells have a long slit for the entrance and the living volutes prey mainly on other molluscs and marine invertebrates. Although oysters are the most famous of the pearl-making molluscs, volutes also create pearls if any grit gets lodged inside their shell. The pearls of the Bailer Shell Volutes are beautiful and can be up to the size of a golf ball and bright orange.

A cosy spot on a rock

Limpets are relatives of garden snails, with a grip strong enough to resist the strongest surf crashing against the rocky shore. They graze on algae growing on the same rocks and often return to the same spot after each feeding excursion – usually at high tide. Often these resting spots are used over and over again for many years by successions of limpets and a depression will form in the rocks, which is just the right size for the limpets to fit snugly into.

Sea-Hare can grow very large and feed on seaweed

Nudibranch

Nudibranchs are brilliantly coloured or strangely shaped sea slugs. Their startling colours are often a warning to predators that they are poisonous or foul tasting, but sometimes it appears to be merely camouflage against their often equally colourful meals of coral polyps, sea anemones, sponges and similar prey. Some nudibranchs are vegetarians and they often resemble the seaweed they feed on, for example the sea-hares.

Octopuses for dinner

Australia has the world's most dangerous octopuses – the blue-ringed and blue-lined octopuses of the genus *Hapalochlaena*. However, there are also many bigger and far less deadly octopus species in Australia. While they all use venom to subdue their prey, they are not a threat to people – indeed some are more in danger of ending up as our dinner! All octopuses usually live for about a year. The females breed only once and then die when their eggs have hatched.

Shape-shifting budgie food

Cuttlefish are the fastest colour-changers in the animal world, altering their texture and colour in 0.3 of a second to blend into their surroundings! They are cephalopod molluscs related to squid and octopus. Cuttlefish catch their prey by shooting out twin tentacles to grab it. When threatened, cuttlefish squirt sepia ink, which is used as a dye – the brownish tones seen in old photos. The white, chalky internal shell of the cuttlefish often washes up on the beach and is used as a treat for pet Budgerigars.

Big squid is watching

The Giant Squid is actually the largest invertebrate in the world, growing up to 13 metres long. It also has the largest known eyes in the world – 25 centimetres in diameter.

The Giant Cuttlefish is the largest cuttlefish in the world – growing to almost one metre long!

Monotremes

Australia also boasts two of the world's three species of monotreme (egg-laying mammals) – echidnas and platypuses. They are two of the most fascinating creatures on Earth. Monotreme means 'one hole', referring to the animal's cloaca, a single opening used for both reproduction and excretion.

One of a kind

The Platypus is the world's only aquatic monotreme. It is also the only venomous monotreme. Male Platypuses have spurs on their hind legs, which produce powerful venom. These can inflict extremely painful wounds in humans, while the venom is capable of killing another smaller animal. Platypuses swim with their ears and eyes closed, but are sensitive to electrical discharges coming from their prey. This enables them to locate the worms, yabbies, tadpoles and other tasty treats, even if they're hidden.

The Platypus is an inhabitant of clean creeks, rivers and streams in south-eastern Australia

Echidnas are found almost anywhere where ants are in Australia, except in the heart of cities and towns

Shy but spiky balls

There are two species of echidna. Short-beaked Echidnas are the Australian species. Sometimes called Spiny Anteaters, their diet is primarily ants – although they will eat termites too. Female echidnas lay one egg and carry it in their pouch until it hatches. The babies start out the size of a jellybean, but grow in the pouch until they start to develop spines. When frightened, echidnas curl into a ball with these sharp spines sticking out to deter predators. Long-beaked Echidnas are found only in New Guinea, where they feed mainly on earthworms.

One hole wonders

Monotremes are the only living mammals that lay eggs. The females have no nipples but provide milk for their young from glands under their skin. It oozes onto a patch of fur, where the babies lap it up. The Platypus is the only member of its family (family Ornithorhynchidae), but there are two species of echidna (family Tachyglossidae) – one found in Australia and New Guinea, and a second in New Guinea only.

Night Birds

This is a grouping of often unrelated birds that are usually active by night and are encountered or heard in the dark. The more familiar night birds are owls and nightjars, but other birds like the 'thick-knees', or bush curlews, are also included. Night birds can be found in both suburban and bushland areas, but most are more often heard than seen.

Curlew

Curlews have eerie calls that sound like drawn-out versions of their name. There are five different Australian birds called curlews, from two unrelated families. Three are true migratory curlews in the sandpiper family, which breed as far away as Siberia or North-East Asia, but spend the winter – our summer – in warmer spots like Australia. The other 'curlews' are nocturnal waders and often called 'Thick-knees', to distinguish them from the true curlews.

Owlet Nightjar

Owlet Nightjars are Australia's smallest night birds – only about 23 centimetres in length. They hunt moths and other nocturnal invertebrates, which they catch either on the wing or on the ground. They fly quietly because they have fringed feathers like true owls. Unlike many nocturnal animals they have little or no reflective eye-shine, making it hard to detect them by torchlight.

Owlet Nightjars fly quietly to catch food on the wing

Barn Owls can find mice in total darkness by listening for them

Who? Who?

Australia has ten species of owl – six masked owls (genus *Tyto*) and four hawk owls (genus *Ninox*). The biggest is the Powerful Owl, large enough to catch possums. The smallest is the Boobook Owl. The Barn Owl is one of the most widely distributed birds in the world, found on all continents except Antarctica. All owls are predators and do most of their hunting at night. Their strong clawed feet have two toes forwards and two backwards, giving them a firm and lethal hold on struggling prey.

Tawny Frogmouth

Tawny Frogmouths (*Podargus strigoides*) are not owls but giant nightjars. The huge mouth is what gives this group of birds their name and the fringe of whisker-like feathers around the beak helps to direct food into the mouth. If you are not sure if you have found an owl or a frogmouth try to pick it up. If it bites you with its huge wide mouth then it's a frogmouth, but if it clutches you with sharp claws then it's an owl!

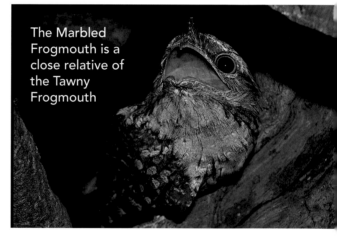
The Marbled Frogmouth is a close relative of the Tawny Frogmouth

The Boobook Owl rests quietly by day

Boobook Owl

Boobooks are Australia's smallest owls, found right across the country. Their prey is similarly small, consisting of large insects, small reptiles, mammals and birds. They rest quietly in the tree branches by day and are usually overlooked by predators and prey alike, but as night falls the familiar 'boobook', 'mopoke' or 'morepork' call can be heard even in the suburbs. Close relatives can be found in New Zealand, Norfolk Island and New Guinea.

Parrots

Australia is a world hotspot for parrot diversity. There are 52 species of parrot, most of which are not found anywhere else. Australian parrots range in size from the tiny Fig Parrots and Budgerigars to the huge Palm Cockatoos, around 60 centimetres in length. Their tough curved beaks allow them to easily crack the plant seeds, which are the main diet of most. Lorikeets feed mainly on nectar and pollen, while cockatoos can chew apart quite large branches to get at the wood-boring grubs inside.

The markings on the head of the Double-eyed Fig Parrot resemble an extra pair of eyes when viewed from the front

My favourite food is figs

Fig Parrots are Australia's smallest parrots – much smaller than Budgies. They love to eat figs, but also take other fruits, berries and seeds, as well as nectar and occasional beetle larvae, gouged out of rotten wood. The species in Australia is the Double-eyed Fig Parrot, which has markings below the eyes that look like another pair of eyes. It distribution is patchy and confined to rainforest, wet eucalypt forest and vegetation along water courses.

Colours

Parrots are thought to have originated in wet forests and as a result they are often green in colour, but in Australia many of our parrots adapted to different habitats and come in colours ranging from pure white to pure black.

Rainbow Lorikeets are colouful, noisy nectar eaters

Sweet-eating Lorikeet

Lorikeets are nectar and pollen feeding parrots. Usually brightly coloured and noisy, these birds fly swiftly through the trees in flocks, seeking out blossom – especially eucalypt blossom – to feed on. They have strange toothbrush-like tongues to help lap up the nectar from the flowers. The six lorikeet species are predominantly green, but have varying amounts of red, orange, yellow and even purple depending on the species. The parents raise their chicks in hollows of tree branches.

A rainbow of budgies

The Australian Budgerigar is the most popular pet bird in the world. Quite a scoop for a small, green and yellow, arid zone parrot! In the wild, it is a flock bird and it is rare to see them alone. They even breed in colonies with every available hollow in a select group of trees or shrubs being used as nests. In captivity, Budgies have been bred to produce a rainbow of colours. They are intelligent birds and enjoy playing with toys and interacting with people.

Perching Birds

Perching birds, or passerines, refers to the order Passeriformes, which contains more than half of all birds in the world today. The main similarity between them all is their feet – they have three toes forwards and one opposing toe on the back of each foot. Perching birds include all the classic bird singers, such as larks, canaries and thrushes, which is why the group is sometimes referred to as Songbirds as well. The largest passerines in Australia are ravens and lyrebirds.

A male Red-capped Robin feeding a tasty insect meal to its chicks

Little Robin Not-Only-Red Breast

'Robin' usually refers to any small insect-eating birds with a red breast. The various robins around the world are often completely unrelated to each other, despite a similar appearance. In Australia there are robins of many chest colours: Scarlet Robins, Hooded Robins, Rose Robins, Yellow Robins, White-breasted and Dusky Robins. The females of most of these birds are duller coloured or plain. Unfortunately many species are declining, possibly due to habitat changes and the increased numbers of predators.

Eastern Yellow Robins eat insects

Hop along currawong

Currawongs are named after the distinctive call of the Pied Currawong. There are three species of currawong, and all have bright yellow eyes and black or grey bodies with white wing patches. They have short legs and tend to hop along the ground – helping to distinguish them from the related Magpies, which walk. They are more at home in the trees and have a strong swooping flight. Currawongs have been blamed for the disappearance of many small birds, as they feed on nestlings and eggs.

Currawongs are close relatives of Magpies and Butcherbirds

Helpful little fairies

Fairy Wrens are very sociable small birds with long tails carried at an upward slant. They are usually seen in small groups of an adult male with several females and young birds. Only the adult males have brightly coloured feathers. They feed close to the ground, picking insects off the foliage. The dominant female of the group builds the nest and lays eggs, but then all members of the group help in feeding the young.

Only the male Superb Fairy Wren has the blue colouring

Perching Birds

Birds of Paradise

Riflebirds, together with the Trumpet Manucode, comprise Australia's four species of birds of paradise. They have loud voices and usually have colourful males with comparatively drab females. Riflebirds mate with more than one partner and males do not help raise the chicks. The females sometimes decorate the rim of their nests with shed snakeskin. Australian Birds of Paradise are found from northern NSW to the tip of Cape York. Riflebirds eat mainly insects while the Manucode is a fruit eater.

Riflebirds are some of Australia's birds of paradise

A female Yellow-bellied Sunbird feeds her chick in their hanging nest

The spider hunter

Yellow-bellied Sunbirds are Australia's equivalent to hummingbirds. Like hummingbirds, sunbirds have colourful males, which defend territories, and inconspicuous females, which do most of the housework! Sunbirds are also known as spider hunters as they commonly seek out spiders as prey rather than insects. In fact, they are often used to control insect-eating spiders in tropical butterfly houses. They also use spider webs in the construction of their hanging nests.

Spotted Pardalote feed on tiny insects high in the tree tops

Pretty pardalotes

Pardalotes feed high in the upper tree canopies, but nest in holes burrowed into the ground. These tiny, colourful birds feed on small insects found on the leaves and any of the insects' sugary secretions. There are four species of pardalotes. Mostly seen singly or in pairs, they do sometimes form small flocks and some species – like the 40-spotted Pardalote of Tasmania – breed in small colonies.

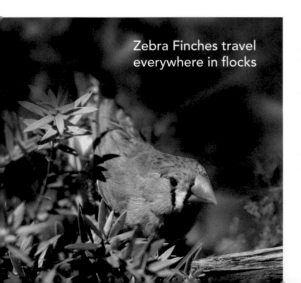

Zebra Finches travel everywhere in flocks

Zebra Finch

Zebra Finches are one of the most popular finches kept around the world yet few people know they are native to Australia. They live in flat, often arid, areas with scattered bushes and lots of grasses, as their main diet is grass seeds. Their nests are usually built in bushes, sometimes in rock cavities. Zebra Finches are very social birds and almost never found alone. Flocks may number in the hundreds. Zebra Finches are prolific breeders and can lay up to 12 eggs in a clutch.

Possums

Possums are marsupials found in every Australian state. They range in size from mouse-size pygmy possums to cat-size cuscuses. There are species that live in tall timbered forests and species that live among rocks. There are quick, slow and gliding possums. Some eat one type of leaf only; others will just as soon eat a small mammal or sleeping bird. There's even one that prefers only nectar and pollen, which very few mammals do.

Home sweet home

Most possums nest in cavities like hollow branches or house roofs. Some ringtail species have gone a step further and build their own comfortable nest in the fork of a tree, like a bird. These nests are called 'dreys'. Other species of ringtail, like the Green Ringtail and the Daintree River Ringtail, live in the tropical rainforests of Queensland. There's even a little known species from the top end, the Rock Ringtail, which lives in rocky boulder outcrops.

Mountain Pygmy Possums are Australia's only alpine specialist marsupials

Mountain Pygmy Possum

The tiny Mountain Pygmy Possum was discovered as a fossil in 1896, but the first living specimen was not seen until 60 years later! The Mountain Pygmy Possum is unusual because it's an alpine marsupial, and Australia has so few high mountainous areas. Unfortunately there are many dangers affecting these possums. Numbers have declined in recent years because of introduced predators, tourism development destroying its only known habitats, and global warming making its mountain homes too warm.

Red hot chilli possums

All seven ringtail possum species are mainly vegetarian, feeding on leaves, buds and flowers of a variety of plants. Common Ringtails are indeed common in many urban areas, as they have adapted to eating a lot of our backyard plants and street trees. Funnily enough, Common Ringtails seem to be immune to the hot taste of chillies and will eat an entire plant on occasion – red fruits, flowers, leaves, and even nibble on the stalk.

What's that smell?

Striped Possums are really stinky! The fact that they're striped black and white like the skunks is no co-incidence, as this stark colouring is probably a warning to would-be predators to stay away. The Striped Possum has one finger on each hand that is much longer than the others, which is used to hook wood-boring grubs and other insects out of holes in rotting trees. Striped Possums also feed on pollen, nectar and tropical fruits.

The long fingers on this Striped Possum are used for hooking out grubs

Pouched Predators

Most people think of marsupials as fluffy little vegetarians nibbling on leaves, but Australia also has some carnivorous marsupials, which are quite fearsome in their own often tiny ways. The largest marsupial predator at the time of European settlement was the now extinct Thylacine, or Tasmanian Tiger. Today the largest marsupial predator is the Tasmanian Devil. There are various marsupial mice, named because of their size, which are voracious predators that would devour a real mouse with pleasure!

A race to the pouch

Quolls are the largest carnivorous marsupials on mainland Australia. They are sometimes called native cats, on account of their size and mouse-chasing habits! Female quolls only develop a pouch a short time before giving birth. In most cases it's little more than a flap of skin covering only six nipples. However, up to 30 rice-sized young may be born after only a 12-day gestation, and those that are too slow miss out and die. This means that only the strongest, quickest ones survive.

Single mum marsupials

Although little bigger than a mouse, the Antechinus are ferocious predators. They catch and eat insects, spiders, centipedes, small lizards and snakes, even small mammals and birds their own size. The females live long enough to raise their pouch full of tiny offspring, but *Antechinus* males are famous for dying soon after mating, which is a prolonged and tiring ritual! This ensures that the aggressive males won't compete with their own young for food and space.

The Yellow-footed Antechinus has a short life if it's a male

A Wongai Ningaui eating a centipede

So what are Ningaui?

The Ningaui are some of the smallest marsupials in the world – some are only 10 centimetres long. Despite their size, these mouse-like creatures are fierce carnivores quite capable of subduing and eating a grasshopper or small lizard much heavier than they are. Their tiny pouch is little more than a flap of skin covering the heads of their babies – usually only 4–7 at a time. When the babies have grown fur, they leave the pouch and ride on their mother's back as she hunts at night.

That devilish Tasmanian

The spine-chilling screeches, pitch black colour and reputed bad temper of the marsupial, led the early European settlers to call it 'The Devil'. Although it can catch and kill its own prey, the feisty Tasmanian Devil is far better as a scavenger. It can devour an entire sheep carcass over time, even eating the hooves and bones. Much of the Devils' spectacular aggressive displays are bluff, to let off steam and avoid more serious fights over food or females.

Tasmanian Devils can eat a whole sheep – horns, hooves and all!

Mysterious moles

Marsupial moles are one of the most elusive marsupials in Australia. They live underground in remote arid areas and rarely surface, usually only after heavy rains. They are blind, with underdeveloped eyes, and their ears just holes in the skin; but they have a good sense of smell and find food by sniffing out small lizards and insects. The moles have silky, golden fur and 'swim' though the sand, using their powerful spade-like claws.

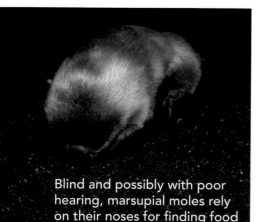
Blind and possibly with poor hearing, marsupial moles rely on their noses for finding food

Evolving moles

Marsupial moles are an excellent example of 'convergent evolution'. Though only distantly related to placental moles on other continents, they are remarkably similar in appearance and behaviour.

Rodents

Rodents are one group of Australian placental mammals. They have two pairs of constantly growing front incisor teeth. These hard, sharp teeth allow them to gnaw away at hard seeds and other tough materials throughout their life, with the teeth growing back as they wear away. Rodents are notorious for producing large families, but most Australian rodents are not as prolific as the introduced species.

The Mitchell's Hopping Mouse bounds around looking for grass seeds

Hopping mice

Although they hop along like tiny kangaroos, hopping mice are placental rodents, not marsupials. They live in small colonies in the Australian desert. By day the mice rest in deep burrows that have a vertical entrance shaft and a number of escape holes, should a predator enter the colony. By night they emerge to feed, covering a wide area with their kangaroo-like bounding. They get all the moisture they need from a dry diet of seeds, but produce the most concentrated urine of any mammal.

White-tailed Rats are as big as rabbits

Who needs a can opener?

White-tailed Rats can reach more than 60 centimetres in length and 1 kilogram in weight and the strength of their jaws is legendary! They can crack open the toughest of nuts, gnawing open even coconuts with ease. Good climbers, they can readily reach nuts and fruits before they fall from the trees, but will also steal birds' eggs and nestlings. White-tailed Rats often chew their way inside dwellings in rainforest areas and have been known to open canned food to eat the contents!

Stick-nest Rat

Before European settlement, there were two species of stick-nest rat – now only the Greater Stick-nest Rat survives. Stick-nest rats build their nests inside piles of dead branches, usually heaped around the base of shrubs. They are vegetarians, feeding mainly on plants with succulent leaves. This sole surviving species was once widespread over much of southern Australia, but introduced foxes almost certainly wiped it – and the extinct Lesser Stick-nest Rat – out on the mainland. It now naturally occurs only on Franklin Island off the South Australian coast.

Stick-nest Rats build large nests of sticks to house their families

The Delicate Mouse is Australia's smallest rodent

Delicate Mouse

These tiny native rodents are found around the northern edge of Australia, where they shelter in simple burrows, feeding mainly on grass seeds. Interestingly, for such tiny and defenceless animals, they are often found in areas with little or no cover in which to hide. With few other rodent species common in these areas, the Delicate Mouse does not have to compete for food. Nevertheless, they are often eaten by owls, snakes and other predators. When conditions are good, the mice can produce a litter every month.

Sea Birds

Sea birds are a diverse group of birds based on where they are found rather than what they are related to. They include birds that fly over the oceans looking for food; birds that swim on or below the surface to catch food; and birds that follow the coasts, seeking food washed ashore or exposed by the tides. In general, most species have webbed feet and are black and white with colourful highlights – mostly red, yellow or orange.

Seagulls

A trip to the beach just wouldn't be the same without the seagulls squabbling over your fish and chips! Seagulls, and in particular Silver Gulls, are the most common sea birds seen across Australia. There are actually seven species of seagulls, ranging in size from the 34 centimetres (beak tip to tail tip) Sabine's Gull, to the comparatively huge Pacific Gull, at 63 centimetres. Gulls are generalist feeders on fish and other marine life either living or dead, washed up on the shore or caught at the surface.

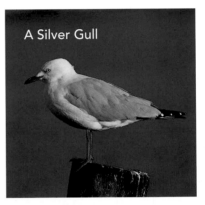

A Silver Gull

Pelicans

'Such a wonderful bird is the pelican, its beak can hold more than its belly can'. In fact, it can hold 13 litres to be precise! Australian Pelicans are large, solid-looking birds, but their skeleton is very lightweight, enabling them to fly long distances. They often turn up far inland, after heavy rains fill waterholes and billabongs and fish become plentiful. Their long bill, with its extendible pouch, scoops fish out of the water rather like a dip net.

Australian Pelicans can be found in inland lakes

RF

Like a shag on a rock

Cormorants are often known as 'shags'. There are five Australian species, which can be found anywhere there is water housing fish, tadpoles or shrimp. They are related to pelicans and have similar feet, with all four toes webbed, allowing them to swim swiftly underwater and catch fish. After they fish, you can see them standing on rocks with their wings outstretched to dry, as their feathers are not waterproof. They make flimsy nests in colonies, usually in trees overhanging water. For centuries in China and Japan, fishermen have used trained cormorants for catching fish.

Black Shags are found in waterways all over Australia

Gannets

Gannets are high-diving, fish-eating sea birds. They are related to Boobies, whose ungainly appearance on land and odd courtship behaviour has led to 'booby' being used to describe a clumsy person! In the air, however, all signs of clumsiness disappear, as Gannets and Boobies are superb divers. They circle above the ocean looking for fish swimming below. Once sighted, they aim and drop like carving knives into the sea, plunging several metres to catch the fish they have targeted.

There is a widespread myth that sailors never harm or kill an albatross, like this Wandering Albatross, as they believe they are the souls of lost sailors

What a wingspan!

Albatrosses are large birds with an impressive wingspan. One species, the Wandering Albatross, has the greatest wingspan of any bird – over 3 metres. These long, slender wings allow albatrosses to glide on air currents for long periods, without flapping their wings. There are about 21 species, but many of those are threatened with extinction. Albatrosses pair for life, choosing the perfect partner with an elaborate courting dance. Pairs breed every second year, producing one chick, which remains in the nest for up to nine months.

Seahorses and Pipefish

Australia has a rich diversity of these Syngnathidae family members: pipefishes, seahorses, pipe-horses and seadragons. The females all lay their eggs in a special pouch or site on the male and he is the one who incubates the eggs and 'gives birth'. Seahorses are at risk from overfishing for herbal medicine, ornaments and the aquarium trade. Luckily they are easy to breed in captivity.

White's Sea-horse is found in Sydney Harbour

What's on the menu?

Seahorses must eat almost continuously to survive. Both adults and young vacuum up tiny aquatic animals and plankton from the surrounding water catch slightly larger prey like small fish and shrimp from the rocks, coral and weed amongst which they live. They are masters at stalking and can drift quietly up to unsuspecting prey and suck it up with a lightning snap before it has a chance to be alarmed.

Upside-down Pipefish

The Upside-down Pipefish is a small straight relative of the seahorses. The pipefish's body is encased in a hard bony 'exoskeleton', like a suit of armour, but unlike seahorses, this species swims upside-down in crevices along the south eastern coast of Australia. Here it stalks and sucks up tiny marine organisms, such as shrimp and baby fish. It has a very distinctive caudal fin, which looks a bit like a colourful webbed foot at the end of its tail!

The Banded or Reeftop Pipefish *Corythoichthys* species

The stay-at-home seahorse

White's Seahorse is found only in Australia and is a common inhabitant of Sydney harbour. They are very territorial and one pair has been observed in a nature reserve, living on the same sponge for two years! Seahorses are extremely slow swimmers and are easily tossed about in the ocean currents. They use their curly prehensile tails to anchor themselves to sea grass, kelp or, more famously, the sharkproof netting around swimming areas at inner harbour beaches, so they don't wash away.

Daddy daycare

Of all the seahorse's incredible features, the most incredible of all is its reproduction. Mating begins with an elaborate dance, in which the male and female twist and twirl about each other, both changing colour. The female then deposits her eggs into a brood pouch on the male's belly. He nurtures the eggs until they hatch and he then appears to 'give birth', expelling hundreds of tiny replicas of himself into the water with each 'contraction'.

The Leafy Sea Dragon is a well camouflaged relative of the seahorses

Seals and Sea Lions

Seals and sea lions are placental mammals, both thought to be related to bears and evolving from the same ancestor. Nevertheless they are different enough to be placed in separate families – the eared seals, fur seals and sea lions in the family Otariidae, are regularly seen resting and breeding around the Australian mainland. The true seals, earless seals or crawling seals, in the family Phocidae, prefer much colder waters closer to Antarctica.

Leopard Seal

This is a true seal with a leopard's spots and sharp teeth. They live in Antarctic waters, amid the ice, where they are fearsome predators of penguins and smaller seal species. They wait for them below the icefloes and snatch them as they enter or leave the water, rarely indulging in high-speed chases. Occasionally a Leopard Seal will wait on land, at a spot where prey are likely to leap out onto the shore, and snatch them before they even know it's there.

Leopard or kitten?

Interestingly, a number of divers have swum with Leopard Seals without being attacked. There ar e reports of the seals catching penguins and offering the live bird to divers, as they might to one of their own young. Leopard Seals are sometimes found stranded, usually sick or injured, on the Australian coast and there is even one record of a live seal being shot quite some distance up the Murray River. Perhaps this helped create stories of Bunyips?

Leopard Seals sometimes rest on Australian beaches if unwell – don't touch them as they can bite hard!

Australian Sea Lions are commonly seen on Kangaroo Island

Australian Sea Lion

The Australian Sea Lion only breeds on the southern coast of Australia. It is rarely seen anywhere else in world. They used to breed in Bass Strait as well, but were harvested to extinction there by the sealing industry in the 1800s. Still comparatively rare due to this past hunting pressure, the total world population is estimated between only 5,000–10,000. Luckily, their breeding spots are now safe and they can breed at any time throughout the year.

A female Australian Sea Lion – males have a darker colour and are much bigger than females

Sharks and Rays

Sharks and rays are members of the vertebrate class Chondrichthyes – jawed fish with skeletons made of cartilage instead of bone. They do not have a 'swim bladder' to help them remain buoyant in the water – they are mostly heavier than water and sink if they stop swimming. Sharks and rays do not have scales but do have a rough protective skin. Some species lay eggs, others give birth to live young.

Ocean carpet camouflage

Wobbegongs are also called carpet sharks because of their beautifully patterned bodies. There are eight species, ranging in size from less than a metre to over 3 metres in length. All ambush passing prey and are masters of camouflage. Their patterned bodies blend in with the background and they have a fringe of fleshy tassels around their heads, which help make the 'dangerous end' even harder to see!

Manta Ray

Despite their relaxed swimming style and considerable size, Manta Rays can jump clear of the water, making a huge belly-flop when they land. They are huge fish (up to 5 metres across) and though related to sharks, are harmless plankton feeders. The fleshy flaps either side of the mouth funnel plankton into their throat where it is filtered by a 'sieve' in front of the gills. They give birth to live young, which may be more than a metre wide at birth.

Manta Rays are gentle plankton feeders

What a whale of a shark!

At 12–15 metres in length, the Whale Shark is easily the world's largest fish. And, like whales, it feeds on some of the smallest marine animals – zooplankton. Whale Sharks wander about the world's oceans, visiting areas where their prey congregates. From March to June, they can be seen in Ningaloo Reef, off the West Australian coast, funnelling hundreds of litres of planktonrich seawater into their mouths. Sadly, the shark fin industry has begun to target this rare species and its numbers are already quite low.

The Whale Shark is the world's largest fish!

Hammerhead fish detective

Hammerhead sharks use their strangely shaped heads as 'hidden fish' detectors. All sharks have special cells that can detect the electric impulses in living animals – hammerheads sweep their heads over the sea bottom and detect fish hidden in the sand. Their 'nostrils' are large and far apart, so they can smell even tiny quantities of scent in all directions. Their eyes are widely spaced too, allowing for a greater field of vision. The winglike shape of the head also gives lift to the shark as it swims.

Electric fish

Numbfish are shocking – literally. There are several species of numbfish, or electric rays, around the coast of Australia. They lie buried in the sand, or swim slowly above it, and electrocute any tasty fishes that venture too close, using electric organs in their fins. They will also zap any predators – or clumsy humans – foolish enough to attack them or touch them. Numbfish are related to Torpedo Rays, which gave their name to the aquatic missile, as both can have a shocking effect on their target!

Snakes

Snakes are reptiles. They have forked tongues, no legs, ears or eyelids, and one of their lungs is either absent or much smaller than the other. Only some species are venomous. All species are strictly carnivorous and hunt their prey either by scent, sight or by heat detection involving heat sensitive pits located around the snakes face. Most species lay eggs but many are live bearers including all the sea-snakes but not the sea kraits. Renowned for the ability of many species to swallow prey much larger than their own body diameter, snakes' diets range from insects, crustaceans, fish, frogs, reptiles including other snakes, birds, and mammals. Although Australia has more venomous species of snakes than non-venomous ones the majority are completely harmless to humans.

Stuck at the scene of the crime

The Brown Tree Snake steals Budgies! When this slender snake was more common, it wasn't unusual to find that during the night one had squeezed into a backyard birdcage, eaten the bird, but then could not escape back through the bars due to the 'bulge' in its body! These are back-fanged snakes and have to open their mouths very wide to strike if they wish to use their venom. They are not dangerous to humans and are usually welcomed for keeping rats away.

The Brown Tree Snake is backfanged but harmless to humans

The Scrub Python, also called the Amythestine Python, is the third longest snake in the world – a specimen 8.5 metres long has been found. Although very long, it is also quite slender and climbs into trees with ease. It then dangles over animal tracks at night and simply plucks prey off the ground as it passes beneath. Tree kangaroos are a popular food item, and it is said that feral cats are not a problem in the Queensland rainforests because the Scrub Pythons eat them all!

When is a black snake brown?

When it's a Mulga Snake! Also called King Brown Snakes, they are unrelated to any of the true brown snakes. They are large, bulky snakes that can reach over 2 metres in length. They mainly feed on lizards and other species of snakes, but if very hungry, they're not above cannibalism! Mulga Snakes are widespread and certainly not restricted to mulga country. The fact that it is a brown species of 'black snake' is important if someone is bitten by these potentially deadly snakes, as treatment with brown snake antivenom would have absolutely no effect!

The Mulga Snake is found in most places in Australia except on the east and south coasts

Snakes

Rough Scaled Snake

If provoked, the Rough Scaled Snake is considered potentially deadly and aggressive, and will repeatedly strike its victim. However, as it is restricted to a few spots around Queensland and northern NSW, bites are quite rare. The venom is similar to Tiger Snake venom, affecting both the nerves and bloodstream, and is treated with the same antivenom. The Rough Scaled Snake is mainly active by day, feeding on frogs, lizards and small mammals. It grows to roughly a metre in length.

Black-ringed Mud Snake

The Black-ringed Mud Snake (Hydrelaps darwiniensis) is a very little known species, despite the fact that it forages for food during the day on the mudflats around Port Darwin in the Northern Territory, which gives it its other common name of the Port Darwin Sea Snake. Most sea snakes are swimming predators that rarely come ashore unless sick or exhausted. The Black-ringed Mud Snake feeds on fish like mudskippers and other gobies found in mud holes at low tide. It is a true sea snake and gives birth to live young rather than laying eggs.

The Black-ringed Mud Snake is a sea snake that looks for food in the mudflats

The very shy Fierce Snake

The deadliest land snake in the world is Australia's Inland Taipan. It has the most powerful venom of any land snake, but, surprisingly, there have been no reported deaths from its bite. Despite also being known as the Fierce Snake, it is shy and reluctant to bite. It also lives only in a very remote area of the black soil plains of central Australia, where encounters with people are rare. This snake needs powerful venom to kill rats very quickly so that it can't escape or fight back.

Elegant Sea Snake

The Elegant Sea-snake feeds on long slender fish of a similar shape to itself, like eels. Youngsters are banded but adults are blotched, as shown in this photo. All the seasnakes have paddle shaped tails to help them swim.

The Elegant Sea Snake is a venomous snake common off the north Australian coast

Spiders

Spiders are an order of the invertebrate class Arachnida. Most, but not all, spiders possess venom glands, two body parts, eight legs and usually eight eyes, and silk-producing glands to make webs and egg-sacs. Some spiders have fangs that are folded parallel when not in use, so the spider must rear up to stab at prey or predators. Others have jaws that work like pincers and can bite without rearing up.

Huntsman Spiders are often found in buildings

Harmless hairy Huntsman

They may look big and scary, but Huntsman Spiders are harmless. They don't build a web, but rest on tree trunks, rocky outcrops and house walls at night and then ambush passing insects. During the daytime, however, these large, tasty spiders must hide or else end up as a meal for a passing bird, lizard or other predator. In the wild, they would hide in rock crevices or behind peeling tree bark, but in urban areas they often seek shelter in houses or parked cars.

Male Red-headed Mouse Spiders are brightly coloured

Mouse Spiders

Mouse Spiders are hairy and live in burrows underground, but that's all they have in common with their cute little namesake! Females spend their whole lives in their burrows, which have two lids to camouflage the entrance. To feed, they ambush passing insects. Males are active during the day, searching for females by following a scent. Males are boldly patterned, which warns predators that they taste bad. Mouse Spider bites can sometimes cause severe symptoms in humans.

Jumping spiders

Jumping spiders can spot their prey from 30 centimetres away, stalk it and jump onto it from 10 centimetres distance – quite a feat for an animal only 12 millimetres long! Male and female jumping spiders have different colours and patterns, so they can tell at a glance what sex another spider is and act accordingly. If they are adults of the opposite sex, the male will put on a courtship display. Judging from the female's reaction, he can tell if she is a potential mate, not interested or in a bad mood and likely to attack instead!

Jumping spiders have excellent eyesight

Putting spiders in order

Spiders, order Araneae, are divided into three sub-orders:

1. Mesothel spiders, which have a segmented abdomen like insects and are not found in Australia.

2. Mygalomorph spiders, which have parallel fangs and need to rear up to strike their prey. This group includes trapdoors, funnelwebs and tarantulas.

3. Araneomorph spiders, which use their jaws like pincers, and includes all the more familiar species like Red-backs, Daddy-long-legs, Garden Orb Spiders and Flower Spiders.

Net-casting spiders

Net-casting spiders have fluffy silken nets that they throw on their prey

Net-casting spiders don't bother spinning large, complex webs. Instead they lurk in low bushes until night falls, then construct a small, furled, rectangular web, which they then grasp between their first two pairs of legs. Below the spider are often some white flecks of spider dropping, which serve as a target. If any prey walks across the white splash, the spider drops down, holding its net wide, and entangles the prey so it can be hoisted off the ground and wrapped up.

Turtles

Turtles, like other reptiles, are scaly. The class Reptilia contains all the lizards, snakes, turtles, tortoises, crocodiles and alligators. Turtles are the only native Australian shelled reptiles. Their hard shell is made of bony scutes covered with large interconnected scales. The upper shell is called the carapace and the lower shell is called the plastron. All turtles lay eggs.

Turtle or tortoise?

All tortoises can be called turtles, but not all turtles are tortoises! A tortoise is a type of turtle. Generally, tortoises live on land, only wading into shallow water to drink and soak. They have thick, flat feet like an elephant, for clambering over rocks and sand, and usually a large domed shell. There are no native Australian tortoises. Turtles are aquatic, spending most of their lives in the water. They have a flatter, streamlined shell and flippers or webbed feet.

The Green Turtle eats seaweed

A Turtle with a beak

Hawksbill Turtles were once killed for their shells, which were marketed as 'tortoiseshell' and carved into combs or ornaments. Hawksbill numbers are in decline and Australia has the largest breeding areas left in the world. Female Hawksbills are very active and, using the claws on their front flippers, can scramble over beach rubble and rocks to reach nesting sites in the sand that other sea turtles cannot reach. These small sea turtles feed mainly on sponges and other marine invertebrates found in rocky reefs.

Shell repairs

If a turtle has a cracked or broken shell, it can be repaired with artificial materials such as fibreglass before the turtle is released back into the wild, good as new!

Sticking its neck out

Most Australian freshwater turtles fold their neck into their shells sideways, a move very obvious in a long-necked species like the Eastern Snake-necked Turtle. All Australian freshwater turtles have a sort of hydraulic swallowing mechanism and an almost useless tongue, which makes eating on land difficult. Snake-necked Turtles use their long necks to reach small, tasty animals like tadpoles and shrimp in the water. They also prove handy as a lever to help flip the turtle right way up, should it fall onto its back.

Eastern Snake-Necked Turtles have bright yellow- or orange-spotted hatchlings

ading Birds

This is a diverse grouping of birds linked by habitat or way of life, rather than genetic features. These are birds that live in or around shallow waters, swamps and mudflats, and seek out food there. Some species are migratory and travel huge distances, while others spend most of their lives in the same general area. Most have long legs and long beaks, adaptations geared to reaching and obtaining food in their watery habitats.

Jabiiru or Black-necked Stork with a swamp eel

Long red legs

The Jabiru is Australia's only species of stork and, at around 1.3 metres tall, it is also our largest wading birds. Although it is also known as the Black-necked Stork, the neck has a green and purple sheen overlaying the black colouring. The Jabiru has a black and white body and bright red legs. It feeds on fish, frogs and crustaceans. The range of the Jabiru has been reduced with changes to floodplains and tall reed beds for agriculture, mining and urban development.

The sacred Aussie ibis

Ibis were sacred birds in Ancient Egypt. One of Australia's three ibis species was once thought to be the same species found in Egypt, so was named the Sacred Ibis. Now it is known to be a separate, but closely related, species and renamed the Australian White Ibis. In the wild, ibis feed as a group, using their long, down-curved bills to probe among grasses and swamps. However, they have adapted so well to city living, that they are now considered a pest.

Egrets

Egrets are any of several herons which are white or pale buff in colour. Some of them also develop attractive hair like plumage in the breeding season. There are five species in Australia called egrets but one species – the Eastern Reef Egret comes in two colour forms – white and grey and only the white form is called a Reef Egret while the grey form is called a Reef Heron! Like all herons the egrets feed on fish frogs, and other small animals which they usually catch in water or swampy conditions. Cattle Egrets are well known for following larger animals and catching any smaller ones flushed out by the activities of the big animals.

The White Ibis is common around many Australian cities

Whales and Dolphins

Whales and dolphins are members of the placental mammal order Cetacea. They are divided into two suborders: the Mysticeti, or baleen whales – the toothless group with baleen to sieve out krill and other tiny sea animals; and the Odontoceti, or toothed whales, which include dolphins, porpoises, Orcas and, the largest of all the toothed whales, the Sperm Whale.

Inland dolphins

While most dolphins live in the open ocean, one species used to be found in Lake Frome in central Australia. That lake dried up long before European settlement and the dolphin is now extinct. Interestingly, it was thought that the Irrawaddy Dolphin, a species that prefers large rivers and estuaries in South East Asia, was found in Australia, but it was a completely new species. It is now named the Australian Snubfin Dolphin, as so far it hasn't been found anywhere else.

Clever, curious killer

Dolphins are small, toothed whales, proven to be very intelligent. Being mammals they also have warm blood and provide milk for their young. The Killer Whale is the largest of the dolphins, growing to almost 10 metres. Although many species are quite shy or live far out to sea where they are rarely seen, some species are very curious and 'friendly' towards people. Most dolphins eat fish and squid but some, like the Killer Whales, also feed on larger prey, including smaller dolphin species and large whales!

Bottle-nosed Dolphins can be very inquisitive

The Humpback
Whale sings very
complex songs

Evolving whales

All whales are mammals. Fossils
indicate that whales possibly evolved
from hoofed land mammals that
started returning to the sea about 50
million years ago. Whale skeletons
show their front legs are modified
into a pair of flippers on their chests
and their hind limbs are reduced to a
few tiny useless bones now fixed in
the body. Their tails, however, are
long and powerful and end in a pair
of flukes to push them through the
waters.

The wrong whales to hunt

Southern Right Whales were named in the early
1900s because they were considered the 'right'
whales to hunt from shore-based whaling
stations. An easy target, they were slow moving,
travelled close to the shore, and had good
blubber layers. So much so, that they were
hunted almost to extinction. They are strictly
protected now, and can be seen along the
Australian coast in winter, migrating north from
the Antarctic to give birth in the comparatively
warmer waters. When spring arrives, the whales
migrate back south, as their calves now have
enough blubber to survive the cold.

Worms

Australian native worms are rarely found in suburban gardens or compost heaps as the pH of the soil and the rich nutrients are often unsuitable for them but one or two do show up occasionally. Most worms found in gardens are introduced species that came into Australia in garden soil but out in the bush there are some very interesting native species.

It's a worm-eat-worm world

There are many completely unrelated animals that are long, skinny and legless that get called 'worms'. There are Gordian worms, Planarian worms, tapeworms, nematode worms – even leeches are a type of worm. Remember that appearances can be deceiving – planarian worms and earthworms aren't related, in fact the carnivorous planarian worms may very well eat the earthworms!

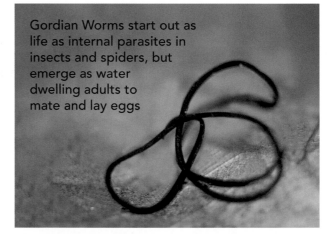

Gordian Worms start out as life as internal parasites in insects and spiders, but emerge as water dwelling adults to mate and lay eggs

Earthworm

Water squirters

Many native Australian worms have another interesting feature – they can squirt jets of watery fluid quite some distance to dissuade attackers. Although it can't actually cause serious damage, the fluid will sting if you get it in your eyes, and it certainly wouldn't taste very nice – a very effective defence against smaller predators! Earthworms are members of the phylum Annelida and are related to leeches, marine bristle worms and Giant Beach Worms.

Big worms for a big country

Australia has some of the largest worms in the world. The most famous of these is the Giant Gippsland Earthworm, which can grow to a length of about 2 metres or more, with a diameter of 2 centimetres. There is another species found around Kyogle in NSW, which, although shorter, grows as thick as a garden hose. Like most earthworms, they feed by breaking down the leaf litter and humus in the soil. Imagine seeing one of those monsters wriggling through your backyard!

Yellow Planarian Worm

The Yellow Planarian Worm tastes awful. It is brightly coloured so that anything that tries them once will remember and never try to eat one again! They live in damp areas and are carnivorous, feeding on small creatures like slaters, which they trap in their slimy trail and then drown with more slime! Land planarians are very good at regenerating if they have an accident. They can also reproduce by breaking into pieces and regenerating.

Yellow Planarian Worms are predators of smaller invertebrates

Activities

Quick Quiz

1. How big are baby quolls when they are born?
2. What do Hawksbill Turtles eat?
3. Are Dingoes marsupials?
4. What kind of insect is a Ladybird?
5. What is another name for the Uca crab?
6. Name four features that you need to be classed as a bird?
7. How wide is the wingspan of a Wandering Albatross?
8. How much can a Pelican's beak actually hold?
9. What is a Nanny-hairy-legs?
10. What is a megapode?
11. How many species of wombats are there?
12. What does a Zebra Lionfish use its attractive pectoral fins for?
13. Are Gang-gangs and Galahs related? If so, how?
14. Do all Australian robins have red chests?
15. What marine stinger is as deadly as the Box Jellyfish?
16. What is a Koala most closely related to?
17. What surprising thing does a Manta Ray do out of the water?
18. What four features would you need to be classed as a monotreme?
19. Give an example of a phylum, a class and a genus?
20. Name three things that snakes don't have?
21. What type of insect are termites?
22. Which Velvet Ant has wings, the male or the female?
23. What's the difference between a yabby and a spiny crayfish?
24. Where do you find octopuses?
25. What is special about the way fish breathe?
26. Where is your dorsal surface?
27. What is a genus?
28. Look up an animal mentioned in this encyclopedia in another book or a computer search engine using *only* its scientific name.

Where Am I?

In which parts of Australia would you expect to find the following animals?

1. Scrub Python
2. Tree Kangaroo
3. Nursery Frog
4. Cassowary
5. White-tailed Rat
6. Flying Foxes
7. Freshwater Crocodile
8. Platypus
9. Ulysses Butterfly
10. Boobook Owl
11. Bilby
12. Stick-nest Rat
13. Mulga Snake
14. Perentie
15. Emu
16. Echidna
17. Dingo
18. Crested Hawk
19. Galah
20. Crucifix Frog

Glossary

arboreal living in trees

bract special leaf at the base of a flower

carrion dead animal flesh

chordates members of the phylum Chordata, which all possess a backbone or notochord

class a group of orders of animals more closely related to each other than to other orders due to shared features

classification the way we determine what species a living thing is, what it is related to and where it fits into the world of living things

crepuscular active at dawn and dusk only

detritovore an animal that eats dirt and disintegrated material

diurnal active during the day

dorsal on the back

echolocation method used by bats of locating objects by listening to the echoes bouncing off them

estuary an area at the mouth of a river or stream that meets the sea

family a group of genera that share some common features not shared by other genera

genus a group of species that share some common features not shared by other genera

gestation the time taken for a baby animal to develop before it is born

gills comb-like respiration organs on aquatic animals, which extract oxygen from water and release carbon dioxide as waste

hermaphrodite having both male and female reproductive characteristics

humus nutrient-rich decomposing plant and animal matter in soil

incubate to keep eggs warm before hatching

invertebrate an animal without a backbone

larvae the grub-like young of insects that look and act differently to the adults and eat different food

marsupial a mammal that gives birth to under-developed young, which are then nursed to an advanced stage inside a marsupium or pouch

monotreme a mammal that lays eggs and has only one body opening for waste and reproduction

nocturnal active at night

nymph the juvenile stage of an invertebrate that resembles the adult in appearance, behaviour and diet

order a group of families of animals more closely related to each other than to other families due to shared features

pectoral on the chest

pedipalps leg-like structures either side of the jaws on some invertebrates

phylum a group of classes of animals more closely related to each other than to other classes due to shared features

placental a mammal that gives birth to live young, which develop inside the mother, with a placenta, which passes nutrients and removes waste via the mother's bloodstream

plankton minute animals and plants that drift about in the water currents. Many are the younger stages of larger animals and plants.

prehensile limb or tail able to hold or grasp objects

rostrum a sharp, hollow, beak-like projection on insects used to feed

species a group of individuals that share common features not shared by other species

sub-phylum a classification slightly more specific than a phylum but less so than a class

sub-class a classification slightly more specific than a class but less so than an order

symbiotic a living arrangement between two different species that benefits them both

vertebrate an animal with a backbone

Want to Know More?

Books

Frogs and Tadpoles of Australia (Second Edition) by Marion Anstis, 2018, New Holland Publishers

A Field Guide to Insects in Australia (Fourth Edition) by Paul Zborowski and Ross Storey, 2017, New Holland Publishers

A Field Guide to Butterflies of Australia: their life histories and larval host plants by Garry Sankowsky and Geoff Walker, 2020, New Holland Publishers

The Slater Field Guide to Australian Birds (Second Edition) by Peter Slater, Pat Slater and Raoul Slater, 2009, New Holland Publishers

A Complete Guide to Reptiles of Australia (Sixth Edition) by Steve Wilson and Gerry Swan, 2020, New Holland Publishers

Strahan's Mammals of Australia (Fourth Edition) by Andrew M Baker and Ian C Gynther (Eds), 2023, New Holland Publishers

A Guide to the Spiders of Australia by Volker W Framenau, Barbara C Baehr and Paul Zborowski, 2014, New Holland Publishers

For beginners the Reed Concise Guide series offers excellent introductions Australian wildlife in a variety of subjects including Birds, Frogs, Snakes, Lizards, Insects, Spiders, Butterflies and Wild Flowers – see **newhollandpublishers.com** for details

Websites

Australian Museum fact sheets and information links: **australian.museum/learn/animals**

Active Wild (this site has many links to pages covering Australian animals): **www.activewild.com/australian-animals-list**

BirdLife Australia (has links to ID pages, conservation projects and citizen science programs such as the Birds In Backyards survey): **birdlife.org.au**

Find-a-spider is a good site that has common spiders and information about them: **www.findaspider.org.au**

If you're interested in freshwater fish then ANGFA is a good society to join with branches in most states: **www.angfa.org.au**

If you want to identify a marine fish this one is hard to beat and is updated regularly: **australian.museum/learn/animals/fishes**

There's a frog society in every state – this link provides information on the frogs and the groups that study them: **frogs.org.au/frogs**

Places to go

National parks in your state or territory are excellent places to visit and see Australian animals. There are also some very good zoos, public aquariums and wildlife parks where you can see them up close. Check with your local tourist information centre to find out which ones are closest to you.

Answers

Quick Quiz

1. Page 98
2. Page 117
3. Page 76
4. Page 25
5. Page 45
6. Pages 54–55
7. Page 102
8. Page 103
9. Page 37
10. Page 82
11. Page 70
12. Page 81
13. Page 39
14. Page 93
15. Page 41
16. Page 71
17. Page 108
18. Page 86
19. Pages 40, 54 and 58
20. Page 110
21. Page 66
22. Page 67
23. Page 45
24. Pages 84–85
25. Page 78
26. Examples: *Coenobita variabilis, Tiliqua scincoides, Bufo marinus, Dacelo gigas, Homo sapiens*

Where Am I?

1. Queensland rainforest
2. Queensland rainforest, in trees
3. Northern Australia, on the ground
4. Queensland rainforest
5. Queensland rainforest
6. Northern and eastern Australia in trees
7. North and north-eastern Australia in fresh water
8. South east Australia in fresh water
9. Tropical northern Australian rainforests
10. In trees anywhere in Australia
11. Central Australia
12. Franklin Island
13. Inland Australia
14. Central Australia
15. In woodland and other habitats
16. Anywhere with ants
17. Throughout Australia
18. In forests of northern and eastern Australia
19. Timbered areas near water
20. Claypans of central NSW and Queensland